The Self-Revealed Knowledge That Liberates the Spirit

Books by the Author

The Path of Light

The Self-Revealed Knowledge That Liberates the Spirit

Living in God

The Book of Life

An Easy Guide to Ayurveda

An Easy Guide to Meditation

A Master Guide to Meditation

Life Surrendered in God
(Patanjali's yoga-sutras)

The Eternal Way
(The Inner Meaning of the Bhagavad Gita)

The Self-Revealed Knowledge that Liberates the Spirit

A Handbook of Essential Information for Experiencing a Conscious Relationship with the Infinite and Restoring Soul Awareness to Wholeness

ROY EUGENE DAVIS

New Age Books

ISBN: 81-7822-050-4

First Indian Edition: 2002

First published in 1997
by CSA Press, USA

Published by
NEW AGE BOOKS
A-44 Naraina Phase I
New Delhi-110 028 (INDIA)
Email: nab@vsnl.in
Website: www.newagebooksindia.com

Printed in India
at Shri Jainendra Press
A-45 Naraina Phase-I New Delhi-110 028

I salute the supreme teacher,
the Truth, whose nature is bliss;
who is the giver of the highest
happiness; who is pure wisdom;
who is beyond all qualities and
infinite like the sky; who is beyond
words; who is one and eternal,
pure and still; who is beyond all
change and phenomena and
the silent witness to all our
thoughts and emotions—I salute
Truth, the supreme teacher.

Ancient Vedic Hymn

PREFACE

In this book I have explained how to comprehend the reality of God and the processes and categories of cosmic manifestation, provided guidelines to living in tune with the Infinite, and described how to have awareness restored to wholeness.

As you read, let new insights be welcomed by your mind and realized at the innermost level of your being. Use your powers of discernment to determine what is true and with intuition access transcendent realities. Avoid thinking or believing that you are incapable of purifying your intellect or of experiencing authentic spiritual growth. Refer to the glossary for meanings of words which may at first be unfamiliar and to more fully comprehend the philosophical concepts and overall theme.

Because you are a spiritual being, complete knowledge of God and of nature and its processes is within you. Your true Self is the immortal, divine essence enlivening your body and mind which will ultimately transcend them. It is your heart, your innermost being, that is to be consciously realized. As soul capacities increase and its innate qualities are unveiled and unfolded, awareness is flooded with insight. Wisdom blossoms, and remains.

Self-realization should not be thought of as an attainment to be accomplished by a few special truth seekers who have exceptional abilities or are singularly favored by a biased deity; it is your natural, free state which you can immediately acknowledge, awaken to, and actualize.

When only that which is real can satisfy your innate

urge to be knowledgeably and functionally free, learn and apply the timeless principles and transformative practices described which have, through the centuries, resulted in the enlightenment and liberation of many devotees of God.

The final knowledge that liberates the spirit is Self-revealed in the illumined consciousness of all who succeed in awakening through the stages of spiritual growth by their focused endeavors and the redemptive actions of God's grace.

ROY EUGENE DAVIS

Spring 1997
Lakemont, Georgia
U.S.A.

Note: Because many readers live in regions of the world where the Western conventional terms "BC" and "AD" are not ordinarily used, when referring to historical events or eras, the more appropriate alternatives "BCE" (Before the Common Era) and "CE" (Common Era) are used instead.

CONTENTS

One

A New Perception of Reality

The heart, the immortal, real Self of us, can only be satisfied with realization of wholeness and complete knowledge of what is true about itself and its relationship with the Infinite. Without this realization and knowledge, we are restless, lonely, and unhappy because unfulfilled.

A mind devoid of confusion, delusions, and illusions, efficiently processes thoughts and sense-conveyed information and welcomes spontaneous unfoldments of the soul's innate knowledge. When mental processes are rational, delusions and illusions are rejected in favor of truth (facts). When Self-knowledge unfolds, it provides *a new perception of reality* that illumines the mind, results in unrestricted flows of soul awareness, and allows spontaneous, wisdom-directed, effective, fulfilled living.

An efficiently functioning mind is necessary for processing a variety of information and for psychological, emotional, and physical well-being. A clear perception of worthwhile purpose is necessary if our lives are to be meaningful and our actions focused. A success-attitude enables us to easily accept good fortune and accomplish worthwhile purposes. Complete dedication to actualizing ideals and fulfilling worthwhile purposes energizes the mind and body and empowers us to more easily make wise choices. It also enables us to disregard or avoid nonessential endeavors and involvements, concentrates energies and constructive endeavors toward essential and worthwhile actions, relationships, and circumstances, and sustains us when we are challenged by thoughts or feelings of uncertainty or occasions of personal difficulty. When only that which is of real value will satisfy the heart that aspires to wholeness, we can nourish the mind with accurate information, nurture the soul with perceptions of truth, and live in harmonious accord with the laws of nature and our innate impulse to be fulfilled.

Our real purpose for being in this world is much different than what is commonly believed. Physical birth, growing through physiological and psychological stages to adulthood, adapting to family and social relationships, and learning survival and functional skills are experiences common to human beings and creatures alike.

Unlike creatures of nature primarily motivated by instinct, human beings, because more self-conscious and endowed with superior mental potential, are inclined to acquire a secular education, learn to work to provide for themselves and others, and endeavor to develop and express their creative abilities. Human beings may also tend to seek excessive sensory stimulation, status, power, and possessions as substitutes for mental peace, Self-knowledge, and God-realization. Most of the actions and circumstances of people who are not yet spiritually awake are but superficial incidents occurring on the stage of self-conscious or egocentric life. They commonly experience their mind-conditioned, habit-bound lives as a partially conscious, dreamlike sequence of events with little or no knowledge of the causes or of how to implement actions to change or improve them.

Our real purpose for being in this world is to awaken to knowledge of ourselves as spiritual beings in relationship to a reality which, not confined by space, time, or relative circumstances, is infinite. When transcendent knowledge is completely unfolded, we can live freely in any realm with purified understanding. When we are fully enlightened, our awareness extends beyond the sense-perceived environment to include all planes and dimensions of the cosmos. It is only the soul's identification with the illusory sense of independent selfhood that limits it.

The space-time realm in which sequential events occur and a seemingly endless variety of circumstances manifest, while illusory, is not an illusion—an unreal phenomenon existing only in the mind of the beholder. It is a continuous manifestation of cosmic forces emanated from the field of omnipresent consciousness we call God.

The cosmos is an undivided, objective expression of a primordial creative energy. When our apprehension of the cosmos is partial, our misperception of the facts is the cause of our personal illusions about it. Illusions that are erroneously believed to be facts are delusions. A few common delusions are: we are mere physical creatures; physical birth is the beginning of one's existence and physical death is its end; some racial types are superior to others; God is an imaginary being believed by some people to exist only because of their ignorance and emotional dependence; there is a malicious or evil force working in opposition to God's will; to aspire to be enlightened is mere wishful thinking; habits cannot be changed; addictions cannot be completely overcome; some circumstances cannot be improved; some illnesses cannot be healed.

Illusions and delusions are the primary causes of

ignorance and its consequences: limitations, misfortune, and suffering. In their absence, the enlightened soul is knowledgeable, freely and spontaneously expresses innate qualities and abilities, and experiences only harmonious unfoldments of events and circumstances while abiding in the permanent bliss of wholeness.

As superconscious states become pronounced, if commitment to wholesome, moral living and spiritual practice remains unwavering, progress is quickened because of the psychological and physiological transformations that occur due to superior superconscious influences and the more easily experienced actions of grace. Soul forces which were mostly dormant during early stages of unfoldment are enlivened and become increasingly expressive.

When soul forces are awakened, they circulate throughout the body, flow upward through the vital centers in the spinal pathway and brain, purify the mind, regenerate the body, and expand soul awareness. Refinement of mental processes and faculties eliminates psychological conflicts, improves powers of concentration, and enhances intellectual ability. Refinement of the body results in improved health and functional capacities and allows the soul's awareness and powers to be more easily expressive. Whatever can be done to enable soul awareness to more easily unfold is of spiritual-growth value. For this reason, philosophical systems that extol spiritual enlightenment as the primary aim of human life provide practical guidelines for wholesome, moral, constructive living.

To live wholesomely, choose a lifestyle which nurtures and supports health and total well-being. A wholesome lifestyle includes a balanced routine of activity and rest;

a nutritious, vegetarian diet; pure water; fresh air; regular, appropriate exercise; spiritual studies and practices; the cultivation of optimism and other life-enhancing mental and emotional states; satisfying relationships; and meaningful endeavors.

Morality is related to what is right or wrong in matters of thinking and behavior. Right is that which is supportive of the highest and best of which we are capable of expressing and experiencing. Wrong is that which is detrimental to our well-being and the actualization of our highest good. The foundation principles of a moral life include harmlessness; honesty; truthfulness; entirely constructive use of abilities, energies, and resources; freedom from addictions; purity; soul contentment; philosophical inquiry; meditative contemplation; humility (absence of egotism); and compassionate or charitable acts. When these principles and practices are expressed in thought, word, and deed, psychological conflicts are avoided and life is lived with the complete support of nature's forces and its capacities to provide for our welfare.

Our thoughts, states of consciousness, and actions at subtle or more obvious levels, can influence others with whom we are in relationship and the universe in which we dwell. All souls are expressive units of the Oversoul, God. All minds are portions of a Universal Mind. The universe is a play of cosmic forces in which everything that occurs influences the whole.

Because constructive behaviors produce beneficial results, our thoughts, moods and actions should be chosen and implemented with purposeful intention. Thoughts, moods, and actions which are not constructive should be avoided. Disciplined thinking, feeling, and behavior is essential to both success in secular life and to spiritual growth. Regulation of mental and sensory impulses empowers us to master both mind and body, control states of consciousness, and live as we are determined to live in accord with our highest understanding and potential. Because our thoughts are better organized and emotions are more stable when our total lifestyle is goal-directed, it is important that we have a clear sense of purpose and dedicate ourselves to it. When our thoughts, resources, and actions are dedicated to well-defined, purposes, the avoidance of behaviors, relationships, and situations which are not in accord with them is easier.

At all stages of soul unfoldment we need to inquire: "What is the real nature of God?"; "What is my relationship to God?"; "What is the purpose for my being in this world?"; "What can I do to know God and fulfill my soul destiny?" It is better to admit the need for understanding and spiritual growth than to self-righteously believe that we are knowledgeable when we are not. An ignorant, spiritually unawake person who thirsts for knowledge can soon experience discernible spiritual growth. A self-centered, egotistical person, even though somewhat educated, is more likely to remain in bondage to ignorance of the truth about transcendent realities until a crisis creates an opportunity for self-examination and a change of viewpoint or a spontaneous spiritual growth episode occurs. A self-centered, deluded person will eventually experience psychological transformation and awaken to awareness of spiritual realities because of the soul's innate urge to have awareness restored to wholeness.

If, in spite of our best efforts, spiritual growth is not evident, it can be helpful to inquire: "What prevents me life, power, and expressive substance evident as and in all that is manifested, and how and why its actions and influences produce effects.

- What we are in relationship to God.
- How to live effectively and successfully.
- How to most efficiently and rapidly actualize (demonstrate or express) authentic spiritual growth that culminates in the complete unfoldment of innate potential, mental illumination, and liberation of consciousness.

To be authentic, spiritual growth must result in illusion-free understanding, orderly soul-mind-body interactions, appropriate, constructive behaviors, and improved personal circumstances. Purified awareness is always psychologically transformative, and valid (well- reasoned) dependable knowledge acquired from reliable sources and Self-revealed knowledge can always be demonstrated in practical ways. Spiritual growth can therefore be immediately verified by the beneficial changes that one experiences and the pronounced functional abilities that can be expressed. The most satisfying results of Self realization are mental serenity and permanent soul contentment.

Awakening to Realization of Absolute Reality

Planet Earth is but our temporary abode. Our true origin is inner space, the transcendent field of unmodified Consciousness-Existence from which we emerged into the realm of nature and to which we are destined to return. Even while we are embodied, the field of Consciousness-Existence is accessible to us whenever we turn attention to it by the actions of prayer, contemplative from knowing the truth about my real Self and God?" a "Why, when I intellectually know the basic facts of life I persist in thinking, feeling, and behaving like a m conditioned human being instead of like the free sp am?" A question that demands of us total self-hones "Of what mundane value is it to me to continue to ex as a spiritually unawake person?"

Common obstacles to spiritual growth are: (1) scious or unconscious desire to remain "only hum the purpose of having the approval of others; (2) t nation to acquire or maintain comfortable or se secure circumstances or personal relationships temporarily satisfy physical and emotional need not soul-satisfying.

Another self-generated obstacle to spiritua the habit of dramatizing emotional immaturity by persistent thoughts and feelings of being u good fortune and a conscious, satisfying God-r When we are personality-centered and do n better, we may think that we can be excused ish behavior. When informed of the truth– spiritual beings, literally an image and like to allow Self-limiting moods and thoughts dramatize narcissistic self-indulgence wh awareness in bondage to irrational ideas, piness, and contributes to dysfunctional their predictable results.

Progressive awakening through the s growth is made easier by acquiring accu about four basic matters:

- The supreme Reality-Being referre

meditation, or by mere acknowledgment. At our innermost level of being we are always established in Consciousness-Existence. When we clearly apprehend it, we know that it is not an ultimate state to be attained nor is any intervening agency needed to enable us to be aware of it. When it is not clearly apprehended, we may be inclined to consider it to be other than our essential condition. We may then also need helpful instruction and supportive guidance until our innate, intelligence-directed urge to have awareness restored to wholeness is sufficiently influential to facilitate the awakening process. Helpful instruction and supportive guidance can be provided by referring to the writings of knowledgeable people who are awake to Self-knowledge and God-realization.

Most useful, is a personal relationship with an enlightened teacher whose words are potent with realization and whose illumined consciousness can be directly transmitted. When we are intent on the spiritual path, providence (divine support and influence) provides us with information, assistance, circumstances, and timely events that light our way and propel us to fulfillment in God. We have to learn to recognize spiritual growth opportunities and prepare ourselves to be receptive to them.

While a wise teacher's words, presence, and obvious or subtle help can be of great value, we must do what we are capable of doing to help ourselves to higher understanding and spiritual freedom. Not all spiritual masters and saints who have appeared on the world scene through the centuries have been acknowledged or understood, and some have been deified and worshipped by intellectually deficient, emotionally dependent devotees who chose to admire rather than become like them.

Anyone who is sincerely inclined to awaken to knowledge of God can do so. All that is required is resolved choice, willingness to learn, and dedicated participation with impersonal, universal causative principles and natural spiritual growth processes that can produce desired results. Because causative principles are impersonal and universal, they can be effectively applied by anyone, anywhere, anytime. Because spiritual growth processes are natural, they can be experienced by any truth seeker who is sensitive enough to be receptive and responsive to them.

For a highly motivated person, oppressive personal circumstances that exist when starting on the awakening path are of little consequence. With learning and spiritual growth, circumstances are certain to be changed to conform to the devotee's higher understanding and constructive actions. What has been done or experienced in the past need not be limiting. As soon as a decision to live a purposeful, God-centered life is firmly resolved, a new cycle begins as causative choices and actions produce entirely constructive effects. The truth seeker, now a disciple (learner), is born anew to a life of almost limitless possibilities for growth and discovery.

When the mind and body have been sufficiently prepared, advanced meditation processes can be learned and regularly practiced for the purpose of quickening the spiritual growth process. The actions of inward grace will also spontaneously effect necessary changes. Interludes of surrendered prayer and contemplative meditation, and practices to become increasingly aware of the presence of God at all times, are easily learned and suitable for everyone at all stages of spiritual growth. For more intentional meditative endeavor, specific meditation techniques and focused contemplation can be practiced.

Advanced procedures are best learned from a selfless, knowledgeable, spiritually conscious person who is a proficient and accomplished meditator and whose enlightenment is obvious. Because the aspiration of the heart is for complete enlightenment and liberation of consciousness, we should choose only the most illuminating teachings, the most practical and useful procedures, and the teacher whose life demonstrates excellence in every way. Desire for magical processes and fascination with fanciful theories should be renounced. Involvements with charismatic or persuasive individuals who make extravagant claims about their spiritual attainment, abilities, or teachings, whose personal delusions are obvious, or whose self-interest is the primary motivation for attracting a following, should be avoided. It is best to allow into our mind and consciousness only that which is true and pure.

When we are new on the spiritual path, our psychological states and intellectual capacities usually determine our approach to Self-discovery. Some truth seekers are inclined to be devotional. Others are more inclined to engage in intellectual inquiry for the purpose of discerning the reality of God, themselves, and nature. The way of selfless service may be most appealing. Many are attracted to the personal benefits and spiritual growth opportunities that attentive meditation practice can provide. For best results, I recommend a well-informed, balanced approach of devotion, intellectual inquiry, selfless service, and meditation practice supported by wholesome, moral, purposeful, constructive living as being most beneficial. With meditation as the foundation routine, all other actions will be more efficient and personal circumstances will be improved.

Meditation that results in experience of superconscious states removes soul awareness from physical, mental, and emotional conditions and establishes it in conscious awareness of pure being. After an interlude of sustained superconscious meditation, it is easier to be soul-centered, make right choices, relate effectively to others and to circumstances, and to live more effectively and successfully. When meditation is not practiced, discontent and restlessness may incline the mind to be excessively involved with external matters. One may then temporarily forget the soul's relationship with the Infinite and revert to involvement with conditioned mental states, habitual behaviors, convenient relationships, and situations that may not be most favorable to overall well-being and spiritual growth.

Some people, inclined to protect their self-centered attitudes and with behaviors influenced by habits and moods, err in thinking that spiritual growth processes have changed through the centuries or that cultural circumstances determine them. One common misguided notion is that in our modern era the average person's sense of individuality and assertive inclination to demonstrate self-determined independence requires a different relationship with the truth teacher: one that might make possible the acquisition of higher knowledge and rapid spiritual growth while allowing the preservation of the self-centered condition. Insightful analysis of this irrational idea will reveal that ego-fixated self-consciousness and illumination of consciousness cannot coexist.

Unlike invalid theories and passing fads that emerge and dissolve into obscurity, the fundamental laws of consciousness are timeless and reliable. God remains ever the same. Lack of spiritual awareness is the primary cause of human suffering. The way to peace of mind, overcoming misfortune, and authentic spiritual growth is that of awakening to Self-knowledge and God-realization.

The following actions are helpful to removing the soul's awareness from attachments to externals and delusions and illusions: (1) experiencing sequential stages of conversion (a gradual or sudden shift of viewpoint that allows perception of higher possibilities); (2) repentance (turning away from all that restricts soul awareness while directing attention and behaviors to that which frees it); (3) commitment to constructive living and spiritual practice; (4) right endeavor to effect psychological transformation and actualize spiritual growth.

Those who desire a casual relationship with a guru (a teacher capable of imparting knowledge and transmitting truth-consciousness) or an enlightenment tradition, are like voyeurs who enjoy observing the object of their interest from a hidden vantage point or dilettantes whose participation is superficial and amateurish. They are not sincerely interested in learning how to grow spiritually. If allowed personal access to a teacher, they waste the teacher's time and energies as well as their own. If allowed to associate with sincere devotees, their presence and behaviors are almost certain to be disruptive and nonsupportive of worthwhile accomplishments for themselves or for others. Like the person described in the following story, they are incapable of recognizing truth when they have access to it:

> A man who had traveled widely in a quest for knowledge, met and talked with many wise teachers. Repeat-

edly, he was informed, "God alone is real; all else is insubstantial and transitory. At the innermost core of your being you are pure consciousness. Realize *that* and you will be free."

"Surely," he told himself, "there must be more to attaining enlightenment than what I have been told."

Continuing his search, he was finally accepted as a disciple by a guru. After a decade of service in the ashram and practice of preparatory disciplines, his guru consented to instruct him in higher knowledge.

"God alone is real," the guru said. "All else is insubstantial and transitory. At the innermost core of your being you are pure consciousness. Realize *that* and you will be free."

The disciple exclaimed, "I've been for here ten years, anxiously waiting for your instruction! Is that all you have to say?"

The guru quietly replied, "Truth has not changed in ten years."

Whether engaged in philosophical reflection, devotional prayer, meditative contemplation, or routine duties, relationships, and circumstances, remember that you are not a mere mortal creature aspiring to an imaginary divine condition; you are an immortal, spiritual being only temporarily relating to the human condition. You are destined to fully awaken in God.

Two

Comprehending the Reality of God

The beginningless, endless reality of God transcending nature is Supreme Consciousness: the Absolute, the field of pure, changeless being. The active, expressive aspect of Supreme Consciousness is the Godhead, the Oversoul with polarity and characteristics which make possible the emanation of a creative force—Om, the primordial-energy-sound-current. Om is the Word that becomes substantial when manifested as nature pervaded by intelligence that controls or regulates the processes occurring in it.

Our aspiration to comprehend the reality of God may conflict with our hesitation to do so. Although we are strangely fascinated by the prospect of confronting the truth about God, we may at the same time fear the consequences: that such revelation might remove us from normal circumstances with which we have become familiar.

Because the Absolute cannot be known by the senses or intellect, the most abstract aspect of God most people are capable of imagining is the Oversoul, and even it remains a noumenon, an object of interest that can only be intuitively apprehended.

It is more common for God to be thought of as a superior person similar to human beings but with characteristics of omnipresence, omnipotence, and omniscience. For many truth seekers, during their early stages of spiritual inquiry and practice, a personalized concept of God is meaningful because it enables them to sense a relationship with something larger than themselves.

The word *god* can be traced to Germanic and Indo-European languages, in which a corresponding ancestor form of the word means "invoked one." The surviving non-Germanic relative is Sanskrit *hu*, used to invoke the gods; in the *Rig-Veda*, the most ancient of the Vedic scriptures: *puru-hutas*, "much invoked," referring to Indra, the god or controlling power of rain and thunder.

God is commonly thought of as a caring father, a nurturing mother, the lord or ruler of the worlds, or as a formless, all-pervading supreme being. Some refer to the Absolute as the male aspect of God, and God's creative energy or *shakti* expressing as nature as the female aspect. As knowledge of God is Self-revealed, concepts of and opinions about God are replaced by actual realization of the truth about God.

Believing God to be omnipresent, omnipotent, omniscient, and benevolent is reassuring and comforting. With this belief (or conviction, if our awareness of God is pronounced) we can also have faith that no matter how difficult or chaotic our personal, social, or global conditions may be, God can and will eventually harmoniously adjust them so that everything will be brought to a happy conclusion. This simple trust can nurture hope and elicit confidence until clear comprehension of the reality of God is acquired and knowledge replaces belief.

The full reality of God cannot be described with words. God is everywhere-present, all-powerful, and all-knowing, and there is an attracting, redemptive aspect of God which can be described as love. We are not accurate if we say that "God is love." Nor are we accurate if we say that God is light, energy, or any other aspect or characteristic we might be capable of perceiving or imagining. Just as attributes of anything (wetness of water, heat of fire, drying influence of air) are not the thing itself, so attributes of God are not God. While certain aspects of God may appeal to us and be the means for our approaching God for the purpose of relationship, when we comprehend the reality of God we know it to be other than the aspects to which we were attracted.

God is sometimes referred to as the first cause, the primary mover that produces effects because of "motiveless necessity." God, being self-complete, cannot be in need of improvement or be bored or restless. God, being the source of the manifesting energy-force that emanates the universe, cannot be in need of change or transformation. God, being the reality of souls, cannot be in need of further enlightenment.

Until we are awake to higher knowledge, our mind-originated explanations of why God produces universes are incomplete. God produces universes, and energizes, sustains, and dissolves them because it is characteristic of God to do so. Thus the "necessity" which impels the cosmos and its actions. Because there is no specific desired or intended outcome, there is no motive for producing universes. Some seers have declared the purpose of the universe to be to serve God's will. The word *will* should be understood as the "inclination" of the impulse of Supreme Consciousness, as the Oversoul, to express.

An agnostic (Greek *agnostos*: *a*, not; *gnostos*, known) does not disbelieve in God but declares there to be no proof of God's existence. An atheist (Greek *atheos*: *a*, not or without; *theos*, god) denies the existence of God. A dèist (deism, Latin: *deus*, god) believes that God created the universe but is withdrawn from it and provides no supernatural revelation. Devotees aspire to God-realization. Spiritually accomplished devotees are established in Self-revealed knowledge of God. The way to satisfy the rational mind and the aspiring heart is to awaken to conscious awareness and experience of God. Until God-realization is actualized, the soul, feeling and believing itself to be separate from God, cannot comprehend the wholeness of God's reality.

Because knowledge is innate to consciousness, at the core of our being we know the reality of God and the processes of the cosmos. Three ways to be *consciously* knowledgeable are (1) to intellectually examine the facts explained by someone who is enlightened or as they are discovered by ourselves; (2) to test what is learned to prove it by personal experience; (3) to have direct, intuitive perception.

The intellectual process can proceed in various ways. We can infer the existence of God by the obvious fact that the universe and its actions must have a cause: something must have produced it and is sustaining it. We can start with known facts and use logic to reasonably conclude that God must exist. We can determine what is true by discarding what cannot be true. The most precise way is to use our powers of discriminative intelligence to see through all appearances, delusions, and illusions to what is true. The intellectual approach is not always possible for everyone because the powers of reason and discernment may not be fully developed. Even so, it is helpful to examine the discoveries of knowledgeable people. Intellectual capacities can then be increased and rewarding episodes of sudden insight will be more common.

The way of verifying knowledge by experimental application is especially satisfying because it allows personal experience which enhances well-being, improves circumstances, and enables one to more easily progress through the stages of personal development and spiritual growth. If knowledge is to be of value to us, we must be able to demonstrate it. To only know about God, the functional laws and principles of nature, and our spiritual identity and ultimate, destined enlightenment, is to be well-informed but may not be empowering or transformative. When we really *know* the reality of God, how the laws and principles of nature work, and what we are in relationship to the Infinite, our knowledge is spontaneously actualized in all aspects of our lives.

Direct comprehension of the reality of God can be realized by regular practice of meditation and meditative contemplation. The most effective way to meditate is to be still, in a quiet place, and withdraw attention from environmental conditions, sense perceptions, and thought processes while remaining conscious, alert, and attentive. When attention is thus internalized, we experience pure awareness, our real nature. Meditative contemplation—an undisturbed flow of attention to the object of concentration—can then be practiced. Meditative contemplation may be practiced for the purpose of comprehending the reality of God or for experiencing transcendent states of consciousness, or both. By surrendering the sense of independent selfhood, the reality of God may be immediately experienced and comprehended.

Meditation proficiency can be acquired by practice.

While some devotees are able to easily internalize their attention and experience spontaneous unfoldments of superconscious states, most people who try to meditate find it difficult to relax the body, overcome restlessness, and quiet their active mental processes. Curiosity about possible outcomes of meditation practice, aspiration to experience clear states of consciousness, devotion to practice, and the application of time-tested procedures such as regulating breathing rhythms, prayer, and directing the body's vital forces upward to the higher brain centers, can be helpful. The effective use of specific psychophysiological (mind-body) techniques can also enable a meditator to experience rapid progress.

When made aware of the precariousness and uncertainty of human existence, and informed of their capacity to unfold their innate potential and be knowledgeably functional in an unbounded universe, we might presume that reasonably intelligent people would want to be God-realized. Presented with a choice between ignorance or knowledge, discontent or happiness, sickness or health, poverty or affluence, anxiety or peace of mind, fated involvement with changing circumstances or conscious immortality, the wiser decision should be easy to acknowledge and make. That the more liberating choice is not always readily perceived—or is actively resisted when it *is* intellectually or intuitively discerned—is a problem that has been examined for centuries by philosophers, theologians, and individuals in the midst of crises.

The primary causes of unknowing and ineptitude are delusions, illusions, and complacency or inertia, all of which are the result of the soul's excessive identification with ego-awareness: its false sense of independent existence. Egoism contracts and confines the soul's awareness, restricts its perceptions of transcendent realities, and inclines it to be attached to mental processes, emotional states, sensory perceptions, physical states, relationships, and circumstances.

Some obstacles to spiritual growth are:

- Inability to learn, intellectual deficiency, or severe mental, emotional, or physical impairment.
- Disinterest, or insufficient desire to know.
- Habitual addictive or dysfunctional behaviors.
- Desire for spiritual growth frustrated by insufficient knowledge to fulfill it.
- Desire for spiritual growth and knowledge of how to effectively accomplish it thwarted by misdirected or inattentive endeavor.
- Reluctance to confront the truth when information about it is provided or when it is Self-revealed.
- Refusal or inability to surrender habitual, egocentric states of self-consciousness which restrict the orderly unfoldment of superconscious and transcendent states of consciousness.

The final solution to all human problems is spiritual enlightenment: mental illumination and unfoldment of conscious knowledge of ourselves as spiritual beings abiding in the wholeness of God. Even though this has been proclaimed by seers for thousands of years and is known in the heart of every person, what it is like to be enlightened may be difficult to imagine and awakening to it may be believed to be difficult or impossible. To make spiritual awakening easier, what is needed is a radical change

overly identifies with a role which is supposed to be understood as a dramatization of a fictional character. When our ego-sense is pure, we know it to be a viewpoint from which we observe ourselves in relationship to objective and subjective circumstances. Thus established in Self-knowledge, we know our personality to be a projection of psychological characteristics through which our soul qualities and abilities are expressive.

While we also need to learn to effectively relate to mundane realms and acquire knowledge that enables us to comfortably live here, comprehending the reality of God until we are fully conscious of living in it, is vital to our permanent happiness and well-being.

> A man, whose life was quite ordinary, received an invitation from a king to visit him at his palace.
>
> Pleased by the prospect of seeing the king and his abode, the man went directly to the entrance of the palace grounds. Walking through the open gateway he was fascinated to see, for the first time in his life, the splendor of the extensive lawns, beautiful flower gardens, and cascading water fountains.
>
> So enamored was he of the panorama, that he completely forgot the purpose his visit. With his mind and senses satiated with his new experience, he returned home. He did not actually get to meet the king or see the interior of the palace, nor in his lifetime did he receive another invitation to return.

In the story, the man whose life was quite ordinary, represents every person who has not yet aspired to Self-knowledge and God-realization, and eventually responds to the urge to do so. The king represents the innermost Self that extends the invitation to be known.

Although the way to discovery is open and nothing bars access to it, the aspirant, who is at first sincerely interested in the prospect of awakening to knowledge, chooses first to examine the objective aspects of consciousness (physical, astral, and causal phenomena) and neglects to go straight to the source of their existence. With the senses now flooded with various fleeting perceptions and the mind filled with nonessential ideas and new memories, aspiration to enlightenment fades. Confused, and compelled by habit, he returns to his normal, ordinary behaviors and circumstances.

Had he used his powers of discriminative intelligence, the outcome would have been different. Had he kept his appointment with Self-knowledge (the king) and become established in it, he could have had free and unlimited access to all of the realms of nature and their varied expressions (the palace grounds) in accord with his inclinations or needs.

How to Know What to Believe

Belief is mental acceptance of or firm conviction about the actuality of something. Do we own our beliefs or are they owned by someone else? By passively agreeing with the opinions of others—be they family members, friends, neighbors, role models, secular authority figures, or individuals thought to have divine insights and powers—we deny ourselves the joy and freedom that personal discovery of knowledge provides.

In matters of religious belief, if we are uncertain of our capacity to know the truth or believe that we do not have the right to aspire to know what is true, we may complacently agree to allow others to determine our actions and beliefs for us.

We should, of course, be receptive to new ideas which emerge from within the wellsprings of our own being and which are communicated by others. The great essential is to thoughtfully examine what we believe, and what we know or think we know, to discern the difference between what is true and what is not.

There are some things we may believe because we intuitively apprehend them to be true even when we cannot yet provide a reasonable explanation. We may believe in God, the essential goodness inherent in others and in nature, and in the assurance of our own immortality. We may have unwavering conviction about these matters before we have actually comprehended the reality of God, perceived evidence of innate goodness, or demonstrated spiritual supremacy over the body, mind, and mundane circumstances.

Read a little; meditate more; think of God all the time.
— *Paramahansa Yogananda*

Three

The Processes and Sequential Categories of Cosmic Manifestation

Universes emerge into objective manifestation from a field of primordial (original) nature emanated by the self-referring processes of an intelligently directed creative energy (Om) which originates in the Oversoul aspect of Supreme Consciousness. The impulse to express arising in the Godhead radiates a flow of energy-force that is modified to produce a field of time, space, and fine cosmic particles with potential to manifest as matter. The Sanskrit name for the field of primordial nature is *maya* (that which measures or defines). Its two influential characteristics are (1) its form-manifesting potential; (2) the effect of clouding consciousness and obscuring the soul's perceptions of its real nature. The soul's involvement of awareness with primordial nature is the cause of its primary delusion which obscures its powers of perception.

Because of its truth-veiling characteristic, in religious literature the field of primordial nature is sometimes referred to as "the darkness." It has also been imaginatively personified as a satanic (Hebrew *satan*, "the adversary") power used to entice souls to remain preoccupied with mundane interests and to avoid knowing God. That this is a mistaken, simplistic notion has not prevented many people from claiming to believe it. Adherence to the

Sequence of Cosmic Manifestation

Field of Absolute Pure Consciousness

Emanation of Consciousness Because of Impulse to Express
Field of God: Consciousness—Existence—Creative Power.

Om

Om Manifesting as Primordial Nature (*Maya*)
Energy of Om, time, space, and essences of cosmic particles
influenced by the gunas: sattva, rajas, tamas.

Field of Cosmic Mind

Eight Aspects of Intelligence of Consciousness in Om
Particularized and pervasive at causal, astral, and physical levels
influential in manifestation, preservation, and dissolution; as All
Pervading Consciousness; and as Reflected Consciousness.

Individualization of Consciousness

Self-Awareness and Ego—the false sense of independent existence.

Intelligence and Individualized Mind

Subtle Organs of Sense Perception

Hearing Touch Sight Taste Smell

Subtle Organs of Actions

Speech Walking Manual Dexterity Elimination Reproduction

Sense Objects

Ether Air Fire Water Earth

erroneous notion that God's will (inclination) can be effectively thwarted by an agent of ignorance serves as a convenient excuse for people who are spiritually passive, intellectually deficient, emotionally immature, or addicted to their present circumstances. It may incline them to disclaim responsibility for their thoughts and actions or to offer unreasonable explanations for the misfortune and suffering of themselves and others.

The field of primordial nature is polarized. Three cosmic forces pervade it and influence and regulate its processes. The qualities or influential characteristics (Sanskrit: *gunas*) of these forces are (1) the positive polarity which is illuminating; (2) the negative polarity which contributes to inertia and heaviness; (3) the neutralizing flow between the two poles which incites to action whatever is influenced by it.

When the impulse within the Godhead to manifest a universe is influential, the enlivening life or spirit of God interacts with the field of primordial nature, producing a field of Cosmic Individuality, the aspect of God at the place between subjective consciousness and objective manifestation. When the light of God's consciousness shines on the field of primordial nature, units of pure consciousness are individualized. The real Self of every person and creature is a unit of God consciousness. Influenced by involvement with primordial nature, units of pure consciousness assume a false sense of independent selfhood: ego consciousness. The soul's awareness, being magnetized, is attracted by the positive pole toward transcendence and toward primordial nature by the negative pole. Thus a mental field is produced: the positive polarity produces the intellectual faculty which makes possible discrimination; the negative polarity produces the mind which processes information.

Five electric currents flow from the egocentric soul as subtle essences and causes of the five instruments of the senses of smell, taste, sight, touch, and hearing; the five instruments of action, excretion, generation, locomotion, dexterity, and speech; and the five objects of the senses which, when united with the senses, satisfy various desires. The fifteen subtle essences and the four components of individualized awareness (consciousness, egoism, the faculty of intelligence, and mind) comprise the nineteen aspects of the causal body or sheath of the soul relating to the subtle material cosmos. It is referred to as a causal body or sheath because it is composed of characteristics which can produce the effects of manifesting astral and physical bodies as the soul becomes increasingly involved with matter. It also enables the soul to accomplish purposes. Causal and astral characteristics coexist with the body and manifest as the seven vital centers in the brain and spine.

Cosmic forces qualified by the qualities (*gunas*) of nature pervade the universe at fine, subtle, and gross levels, make material manifestation possible, and are influential in all of the processes which occur in the realms of nature. As our mental creations exist in our awareness during waking and dream states, so the universe exists in God's omnipresent awareness.

Eight influential aspects of God, seven which are subjective and one which is objective, are expressive in manifesting and maintaining the universe. Six of the subjective aspects, pervasive and specialized, are influential in cosmic affairs at causal, astral, and physical levels to regulate the processes of manifestation, preservation, and transformations of the cosmos.

The seventh subjective aspect is the all-pervading consciousness of God, the *presence* which is most easily accessible to devotees who desire to experience a relationship with God.

The eighth aspect is cosmic, individualized God consciousness which causes the universe to manifest and persist just as our individualized consciousness in relationship to our minds, bodies, and personal circumstances causes them to manifest and persist.

God's intelligence is innate to cosmic individualized God consciousness which produces a Universal Mind and emanates electric currents which, when modified by cosmic forces, manifest as causal, astral, and physical realms. These realms are inhabited by souls which are attracted to them in accord with the causative principle of correspondences: inner conditions determine outer circumstances. Our states of consciousness, mental states, personal interests and inclinations, desires, tendencies, and capacities to discern and to be functionally expressive, cause us to seek out or attract to ourselves the conditions and relationships with which we are most compatible. We are on Planet Earth because it attracts our attention and we are most comfortable and functional here, have lessons to learn, have promises or agreements to keep or a service to perform, or need to further awaken to our relationship with the Infinite.

Because the reality of God is always fully present where we are, we can be knowledgeable, Self-realized, God-conscious, healthy, affluent, and freely expressive and fulfilled in this world. Because the One Mind is our larger mind, it is consistently responsive to our desires, needs, and aspirations, and makes possible their easy fulfillment when we are in a harmonious relationship to it. In accord with our conscious or unconscious desires, Universal Mind effortlessly provides appropriate circumstances. When we are established in Self-knowledge and are in attunement with the Infinite, Universal Mind spontaneously provides circumstances for the satisfaction of our needs even when they are not consciously known by us.

A father requested of his son:

"Bring to me a fruit of that large tree."
"Here it is, Sir."
"Break it."
"It is broken, Sir,"
"What do you see there?"
"These seeds, which are very small."
"Break one of them."
"It is broken, Sir."
"What do you see there?"
"Not anything, Sir."

The father said: "That subtle essence which you do not perceive, is the very essence of this great tree. Believe it. That which is the subtle essence, to that all that exists owes its existence. It is the True. It is the Self, and you are it."

—*From the Chandogya Upanishad*

Four

The Soul's Journey in Time and Space

As sojourners in the cosmic ocean of life, we are fated to wander in time and space and to experience a variety of impermanent relationships and circumstances until, having discovered the truth about ourselves, we awaken from the dream of mortality and fulfill our spiritual destiny.

Our *fate* is what we experience as a result of lack of knowledge and our karmic conditions: our mental and emotional states as determined by our egocentric whims, desires, habits, addictions, clouded awareness, and conditioned psychological states. Our *destiny* is fulfilled when we are in harmony with nature's rhythms, responsive to innate impulses that are inclined to expand our awareness, and the supportive, transformative, redemptive actions of God's grace. Fated circumstances are effects of causes; destined circumstances and events are results of actualizations of the qualities and potentialities of the true Self as it progressively awakens to flawless Self-knowledge and liberation of consciousness.

Our journey began when we were individualized as reflected rays of God's consciousness and became involved with nature and nature's influences. Individualized pure consciousness is the immortal Self. It is referred to as a soul when identified with ego or self-sense and subtle matter. Because knowledge of God and of cosmic processes innate to the Self was somewhat suppressed when awareness was excessively identified with subtle matter, we assumed a viewpoint of independent being (ego-sense). We then began to but dimly perceive ourselves in relationship to God and the universe through our newly produced intellectual and mental faculties, instead of having conscious experience of God and intuitive knowledge of cosmic processes. Somewhat confused, and impelled by the force of inertia to become further involved with nature's processes, we became encased in causal, astral, and physical bodies in order to relate to the realms into which we were impelled or to which we were attracted.

The seven realms of cosmic manifestation and their relationships to the vital centers in the human body are:

- *The realm or field of God*, the Oversoul aspect of God; related to the vital centers in the higher brain.
- *The realm of the Spirit of God*, the sphere of the radiant, enlivening aspect of God; related to the spiritual eye center.
- *The realm of spiritual reflection*, where Cosmic Individualization occurs and rays of the Spirit of God reflected from the field of primordial nature are individualized as souls; related to the vital center at the cervical region of the spine.
- *The realm of primordial nature*, the sphere of Om, time, space, and fine cosmic particles. The "door" between the subjective and objective realms; related to the vital center at the dorsal region of the spine.
- *The causal realm*, the sphere of magnetism, electric currents, and fine essences with the potential to be emanated as subtle and gross phenomena; related to the vital center at the lumbar region of the spine.

- *The astral realm*, the sphere of life forces and electric attributes; related to the vital center at the sacral region of the spine.
- *The realm of gross matter*, the physical universe; related to the vital center at the base of the spine.

The direct way to Self-realization is to withdraw attention from all that interferes with awareness and knowledge of what we are as spiritual beings. This can be accomplished by Self-analysis, intellectual discernment, and superconscious meditation practice. To analyze the Self is to inquire into the essential nature until it is clearly apprehended by intellectual means, intuitively comprehended, and experienced in fact. Superconscious meditation is practiced by directing attention to the higher brain centers to withdraw them from the sense organs and disconnect awareness from physical and mental processes.

During waking states, we are aware of thoughts, emotional states, sense perceptions, and physical sensations. During dreams, our thoughts, emotions, and subtle astral sense perceptions are dominant. When engaged in abstract thinking and during dreamless sleep, we are more identified with our causal body. During meditation, we are consciously identified with our causal body, are capable of exercising intellectual discrimination, and can easily experience spontaneous unfoldments of superconscious states. With practice, we can maintain superconsciousness during sleep and when awake and engaged in activities. By being superconscious we can experience transitions from physical to astral and causal awareness without having episodes of confusion or unconsciousness.

In the physical realm the Self expresses through five

sheaths or coverings. The successive manifestations of these coverings as the soul becomes progressively involved with matter are:

- *The bliss sheath*, the seat of feeling even for a Self-realized being who experiences supreme soul satisfaction while yet somewhat ego-identified. It is composed of fine aspects of primordial nature.
- *The knowledge sheath*, composed of magnetic fields and electricities formed under the influence of the positive polarity; the seat of the faculty of intelligence which provides the ability to discriminate, to determine the truth of what is examined.
- *The mind sheath*, composed of magnetic fields and electricities formed under the influence of the negative polarity. Its five subtle counterparts of the organs of the senses make possible the processing of sense-perceived information and of thoughts. The bliss, knowledge, and mind sheaths comprise the soul's causal body.
- *The life force sheath*, the astral body with the five subtle organs of action and the seven cerebrospinal vital centers. The five element essences function through the five lower vital centers. The sixth vital enter is the spiritual eye, the reflected light from the medulla oblongata. The location of the seventh vital center, the crown chakra, in the higher brain.
- *The physical sheath or body*, referred to as the food sheath because it is nourished by food.

Just as the individualized Self attracts five coverings or bodies, so cosmic individualized God consciousness involved with nature attracts to itself five corresponding coverings when manifesting a universe.

When the subtle manifesting aspects and forces are completely projected, the attracting force of the Godhead becomes influential, resulting in the gathering of elements and the formation of a physical universe with galaxies, solar systems, and planets. As souls awaken and nature is transformed, the subtle aspects are unveiled.

- When the sheath or covering of gross primordial matter becomes less dense and the life forces with their organs of action become expressive, life processes become evident and vegetation emerges on a planet.
- When the mental sheath with its subtle organs of sense perception is unveiled, cellular life, organisms, and creatures comprising the animal kingdom with varying degrees of self-consciousness emerge.
- When the knowledge sheath is unveiled, human beings with powers of discriminative determination evolve on the planet.
- When the bliss sheath is unveiled, the soul knows itself to be a ray of God's consciousness.
- When the final sheath of fine primordial substance is unveiled, the awareness of the Self is restored to wholeness and is permanently free from the possibility of ever again being blindly identified with matter.

The Periodic Processes of Emergence into the Spheres of Universal Manifestation and Our Eventual Withdrawal From Them

The soul is carried into involvement with nature by the outflowing, manifesting current issuing from the

Godhead and identifies with causal, astral, or physical realms depending on the degree of momentum of the manifesting current. Several million years ago, when the first simple life forms evolved, rays of God's consciousness (souls) enlivened them. This does not mean that all souls now expressing through human bodies began their involvement with animal forms. To answer the often asked question, "Do animals have souls?", the answer must be that the life essence animating biological forms are souls. Animals are not self-conscious until they begin to express through bodies with highly developed nervous systems, and then only partially so. They do have capacities to adapt to environmental conditions and to learn survival skills.

When life forms on a planet are sufficiently developed to accommodate a self-conscious soul, humankind begins to evolve. We have no accurate history of the emergence of human beings on Planet Earth. Some estimates are that early humanlike creatures evolved on the planet over two million years ago. It is now commonly accepted by most anthropologists that the human body has not changed very much over the past 40,000 years. The highly developed cerebrospinal nervous system of humans is uniquely adapted to process vast quantities of information, allow rapid learning, and serve as a conduit for higher states of consciousness. So far as we know, humans are the only species who think about such matters as: "What am I?"; "Why was I born?"; "What is the purpose of life?"; "Is there a Larger Reality?"; "What is my relationship to the cosmos and to that which produced it?"

Our compassionate behavior in relationship to animals can be demonstrated by allowing them freedom to fulfill their purposes with as little interference from us as possible, including not using them for food or causing them hardship of any kind. It is not rational, however, to think of animals as human beings in disguise or to consider them our equals in mental or functional capacities.

As souls emerge from inner space to involvement with causal and astral realms, they emanate causal and astral characteristics to enable them to relate to those spheres. Souls entering the astral realm simply emerge there and may be attracted to other souls whose characteristics are similar to their own. To enter the earth realm, a physical body must be provided.

Until the middle of the 20th century, some teachers of esoteric traditions believed that souls were attracted to prospective parents by an astral light generated by their intimate proximity. With discoveries in medical science having made possible artificial insemination and even the joining of a sperm and ovum outside the donors, this theory, although attractive to people who are fascinated by exotic metaphysical explanations which have an appealing charm, is no longer capable of being defended.

Souls identify with the physical realm at the time of conception when a sperm and ovum unite and their states of consciousness and mental states are influential from that moment. They can then be influenced by environmental factors which prevail during the nine months ordinarily required for the full development of the infant body. The basic mind-body constitution of the soul coming into the world is determined by the force of its own consciousness, modified by the mind-body characteristics of the parents and by environmental influences—including the mother's diet, and the general mental, emotional, and physical characteristics dramatized by others who are in close relationship to the mother during the gestation period. At the precise moment of physical birth, when the infant begins to breathe and function independently of the mother, the kinds and qualities of energies at the location of birth as determined by planetary placements and relationships may also be influential.

Many souls, fresh from the astral realm, are highly aware and mentally pure because their subconscious tendencies are still dormant. Many young children have innate knowledge of their true nature as spiritual beings. Unfortunately, for most newly incarnated souls, as they adopt habits, viewpoints, beliefs, and behaviors of family members and others with whom they are associated, their awareness often becomes clouded. They begin to assume a self-centered, human conscious role, forgetting their origin in inner space and their true identity. When their dormant karmic conditions become influential, they may consciously or unconsciously endeavor to fulfill desires and cravings impelled by their urges and compulsions rather than to be constructively goal-directed as determined by intuitive insight and rational thinking. They may be intimidated by others who are addicted to the human condition. Wanting to be accepted, they may deny their own divinity when they have occasional glimpses of it.

Because most children are not fortunate enough to be born into circumstances which enable them to have access to the facts of life at an early age, this knowledge, if it is wanted, usually has to be sought independently. It would be helpful if every child was provided with an environment totally supportive of its potential and with accurate knowledge of God, life's processes, and the purpose of being here. One situation discerning children become aware of very early in earth life, is that most adults are neither exceptionally intelligent nor consistently rational in their thinking or behaviors. The majority of people on the planet today are impelled by their emotions, more interested in self-serving actions and relationships than in Self-discovery, and passively complacent about their present psychological and spiritual states. Their knowledge of higher realities is minimal and their hope of living beyond this incarnation, if they have such hope, is nurtured by blind faith. Although they know that physical demise is inevitable, they avoid confronting it and do little to assure their spiritual growth and future well-being. To them, eternal life is a mere concept, an idea they have heard or perhaps thought about, not a fact that they personally comprehend.

Every young adult should be taught that they have four primary things to learn and do to ensure their total happiness and well-being:

- How to flow with the rhythms of life to be healthy, successful, and have the full support of the universe. To do this, they need to know that there is an enlivening Power nurturing the universe and them, and they can learn to cooperate with it. This can be accomplished by discovering their true purpose in life and fulfilling it by using their skills and talents in harmonious accord with natural laws while being responsive to the supportive actions of God's grace.
- How to think and act so that desires, which should be wholesome, constructive, and life-enhancing, can always be easily fulfilled. To do this, they need to learn to be discerning and to think and act in cooperation with the cre-

ative principles that make possible desired outcomes.

- How to be affluent. Because life, as an expression of a single, conscious Reality, is whole or continuous, unlimited resources are available to everyone. When this understanding is clear and actions are appropriate, resources, circumstances, relationships, and events harmoniously unfold so that personal needs are always spontaneously provided.
- How to experience rapid spiritual growth that culminates in complete awakening to full realization of their true nature and their relationship with the Infinite—which they can do if they sincerely want to. Spiritual growth is not an attainment; it is the result of learning to allow innate knowledge and soul qualities to unfold.

If you were taught, or intuitively knew these four primary requirements for well-being and fulfillment when you were a young adult, you are extremely fortunate.

Because only a few embodied souls, distracted by a variety of alluring circumstances that seem to promise enjoyment or satisfaction, or preoccupied with passing events or self-centered interests, awaken to Self-knowledge during one visit to earth, most usually return many times. Their experiences of repeated physical birth and death continue until they outgrow their attachments to this realm by awakening to higher realities.

Our relationships with the universe are determined by our states of consciousness, mental states, and choices of behavior and we can only perceive and apprehend to the extent of our capacity to do so. Our mental states influence our circumstances, and our wise or unwise actions produce corresponding effects. We are where we are in space-time and our circumstances are what they are because of our habitual states of consciousness, mental states, choices, and personal behaviors.

Considering the matter of fate—the law of cause and effect or karma—we should acknowledge that what we have experienced, thought, and done in the past has produced our present circumstances. Much of our personal history is shrouded in mystery because unremembered. Many of the intellectual errors we made in the past and the unwise actions we performed were the result of our ignorance due to insufficient spiritual awareness. The past cannot be changed but it can be redeemed by coming to terms with past events that are remembered, by awakening to clear states of consciousness, and by implementing rational, insightful, purposeful choices and actions now.

There is no need to try to remember prior incarnations in an attempt to better understand the present one, although spontaneous revelations may provide useful information from time to time. If we attempt to remember prior incarnations we may be inclined to allow false memories, illusional reveries, and fascination with endeavors to unravel the past and discern its meaning to divert our attention from the more important matter of living with conscious intention.

Many people have experienced occasional incidents of conscious separation from the physical body. These are usually unanticipated and may occur during a quiet moment of philosophical reflection, just before going to sleep, when involved in a traumatic accident, during an illness, while undergoing a surgical procedure, or at any other time. One may suddenly be standing a few feet distant from the body, observing it. Or a floating sensation may be experienced, followed by rising out of the body and hovering over it.

Some individuals have reported that, while undergoing surgery or when very ill, they became aware of a tunnel of light in the forehead through which they "traveled" to a light realm which seemed to be pervaded by a benevolent "presence." Often, they report that telepathic or soul-to-soul communication revealed to them some of truths about God and the universe, reassured them, and informed them of their life purpose. They tell of having seen deceased friends and relatives, and sometimes saintly beings. Often, because their perceptions of subjective realities are mixed with mental and emotional states, much of what they experience is modified by their thoughts and feelings. A Christian may see Jesus and his disciples; a Hindu may see Krishna or other hero spirits and gods and goddesses that are believed to exist; a Buddhist may see saints of that tradition. Such perceptions indicate that the contents of one's mind can produce subjective phenomena that appears to be real.

The visionary perceptions reported by persons who have undergone a near-death episode are similar to those reported by meditators who have succeeded in internalizing their life forces while concentrating at the spiritual eye center. One must therefore be very aware and alert to discern the difference between perceptions which are the product of stimulation of brain centers and those which are of a genuine, transcendent character.

Stimulation of the right temporal lobe of the brain, the area above the right ear corresponding to perception, with mild electromagnetic fields can result in similar experiences. Subjecting the body to massive physical stress, severe emotional trauma, sensory deprivation, isolation from familiar circumstances, a sudden interruption of personal lifestyle routine, insufficient nutrition, or an insufficient supply of oxygen can cause one to have perceptions which are similar to those associated with claims of mystical or supersensory experiences. Feelings of security, well-being, and what may be interpreted as love, can occur when endorphins, opiate-like compounds that neutralize pain and alleviate fear, are released by the brain at times of physical or psychological stress.

Whether perceptions of any kind which seem to be transcendent are elicited by physiological or neurological distress or are instances of genuine soul awakening, they are often accompanied by notable changes such as heightened interest in living and feelings and attitudes of unconditional love for all people and creatures. If people who have such experiences are naive—too eager to accept superficial appearances without discerning the truth of a situation—they may not be able to discern the difference between illusory perceptions and those which are the result of soul awakening.

To mistake the unreal for the real, is to make an intellectual and intuitive error that will result in a continuation of irrational thinking and behaviors that reinforce the soul's addictions to mundane relationships and circumstances. For this reason, enlightened teachers recommend that one focus on awakening to Self-knowledge and not be fascinated by perceived phenomena of any kind.

Several years ago I knew an elderly man who lived in the United States and traveled frequently to India to visit his guru. Once, in the south of India, he suffered physical distress and was taken to a nearby hospital for emergency treatment. He later told of being out of the body during that time. He found himself in a room facing a judge who opened a large book and showed him a record of his past incarnations. The man's guru came into the room and asked the judge for permission for the man to stay on earth. It was granted and the man shortly thereafter awoke in the recovery room of the hospital. When the guru was asked by others about the truthfulness of the man's story, he said, "It is true. *It happened in his own mind.*" Then he said, "I was there to guide him through it."

Conscious astral and causal realm experiences can be had by souls perceptive enough to access those realms at will. Fleeting perceptions of subtle realms while one is confined to self-conscious viewpoints and considerations do not completely illumine the mind or consciousness. While it is helpful to have valid information about such matters, it is of superior value for one to be committed to practices that can contribute to psychological transformation and progressive spiritual awakening. Accurate knowledge that enables the fulfillment of major purposes and which provides insight into the wholeness of life will then be acquired by observation, experience, and revelation.

Most souls return here because of their relationships with other souls with similar fates or destinies and because of familiarity with Planet Earth. Some souls occasionally reincarnate on planets in other regions of our galaxy or in other galaxies. The number of earth returns is not fixed. Some souls return thousands of times; others require only a few visits to work out their karma and awaken to levels of Self-understanding and competence which enable them to continue their spiritual growth in astral and causal realms.

After discarding all attachments to the physical realm, astral reincarnation may continue to be experienced, with awareness shifting between astral and causal levels until attachments to the astral sphere are discarded. When the causal realms are completely transcended, absolute liberation is accomplished.

It is not necessary to undergo successive rounds of reincarnation to be liberated. For highly motivated souls, the ideal outcome is to be removed from cycles of causation by accomplishing complete spiritual awakening to the final stage of full enlightenment while embodied. Wherever we are, we have the potential to awaken from delusions and illusions and be free. It is a mistake to think that a different place, a future moment in time, or different circumstances, will provide a more favorable opportunity to be Self-realized. Self-realization is possible the moment we acknowledge the truth about ourselves.

To come to terms with our liberation, we need to confront the possibility directly and do what we can to awaken from the dream of mortality. If we are in bondage to ignorance, the solution is to acquire knowledge. If we are unaware of our spiritual nature, the solution is to become aware of it. If we are not living effectively, the solution is to learn how to skillfully function.

When we sleep we unconsciously die to the world. For spiritually unawake people, transition from the physical body to the astral realm is like going to sleep and waking up in a new environment. After a duration in an astral realm which is compatible with their states of consciousness, they go to sleep and awaken in an infant body on earth to fulfill their desires, accomplish purposes, and eventually awaken to Self-knowledge.

People who are more conscious, experience transition with heightened awareness. Their perceptions of the physical realm fade as astral and transcendent perceptions become pronounced. To ensure continuity of awareness, it is best to learn to experience conscious transition. The best preparation for the future episode of final transition from the body is Self-knowledge, insightful living, and regular superconscious meditation. By living effectively in the multidimensional universe while embodied, functional skills can be acquired and innate knowledge unfolded until spiritual enlightenment is permanent.

While it is a good idea to always be prepared to depart this world, our focus should be upon living a healthy, long life in the body to accomplish all of our purposes, including that of complete liberation of consciousness. For devotees of God, periodic episodes of death and reincarnation waste time that could be better used for living with intentional purpose and often involve them in circumstances which are distracting and meaningless. Most people die because of tiredness, disinterest, boredom, or illnesses or accidents which could have been avoided.

The way to live a healthy, productive, long life is to choose a simple, wholesome lifestyle, cultivate psychological balance and spiritual growth, and have worthwhile reasons to live. People who are confronted by challenges of one kind or another—such as physical illness, psychological unrest, or oppressive situations—who want to solve their problems and get on with their lives, need to do what is possible to help themselves while planning what they are going to do when their problems are solved. Without a vision of possibilities for future well-being there may be a tendency to give up, to assume a role of being a victim of circumstances. As spirit-mind-body beings, our spiritual capacities are superior to mental and physical conditions.

Weak-willed people tend to accept simplistic answers to their questions about the meaning of life and about why things happen as they do. They may be overly eager to believe someone who seems to them to be more knowledgeable or more competent or who is presumed by them or their associates to be an authority. While we are wise to at least listen to others who are truly knowledgeable and competent, we should also use our own intellectual powers to ultimately discern truth from untruth. At the end of our freedom-quest, it is our comprehension of what is true that banishes delusions and illusions.

Theories Regarding Aging of the Body, and Behaviors that Can Contribute to Healthier, Longer Life

Scientists are just beginning to discover some of the causes of aging and how to slow it. A child born in the United States in 1900 could be expected to live 47 years. After 1950, changes were noticed. Life expectancy began to increase at a rate of 2% a year. As of 1997, the life expectancy of a new born infant was estimated to be at least 76 years, with many people certain to live well beyond that age.

A researcher recently took some cells from fetal tissue and transferred them to a culture of nutrients in a Petri dish. The cells divided approximately 100 times, then began to consume less food and their membranes deteriorated. The tentative conclusion was that human cells have a built-in time code that determines how many times they will divide.

One theory regarding a cause for the symptoms of aging is that excess sugars can bind with proteins, forming a sticky, weblike coating that, over time, stiffens joints, blocks arteries, and clouds clear tissues like the lens of the eye, causing cataracts. This idea evolved when it was noted that these symptoms often occur in the bodies of people suffering from diabetes.

One of the processes that makes heavy demands on body cells is food processing. Like all organisms, cells produce waste as they metabolize energy. A harmful by-product of this process is a type of oxygen molecule known as a free radical: an ordinary molecule with an extra electron. The extra electron creates an imbalance that the molecule endeavors to correct by trying to bond with other molecules or structures, including DNA, damaging them. Over many years, this activity can result in specific complications as well as the more generalized symptoms of aging such as wrinkles and some forms of arthritis.

A practical approach to encouraging efficient biochemical function is to reduce food intake. Studies reveal that rats, provided a diet with 30% fewer calories than a control group, tend to be healthier and to live 30% to 40% longer. For human needs, that translates to approximately 1,400 calories a day to result in 30 extra years of life. One theory in regard to the life-extension results of lowered food intake is that, when calories are restricted, body temperature is lowered one or two degrees. Lower body temperature means a less vigorous metabolism, which results in less food being processed. Because fewer calories are available, fewer are burned. When metabolism slows down, so does cell division. It should be understood, however, that reducing one's food intake does not mean that the body should be starved; a nutrition-rich diet plan is recommended while nonessential and excessive food consumption should be avoided.

Several researchers have advocated diets high in fruits and vegetables containing carotenoid: substances that behave like antioxidants by absorbing free radicals. In some instances, this approach has seemed helpful. Other studies, however, have indicated that some antioxidants, such as beta carotene, when taken as supplements instead of in foods, seem to be associated with an *increase* of free radicals. Antioxidants are believed to be most effective when obtained from natural food sources with nutrients which are apparently essential for the body's efficient use of the antioxidants.

In Asia, many centuries ago, a few sages investigated methods for ensuring physical health and long life to allow themselves ample time to accomplish enlightenment and complete their humanitarian service projects. Because of their research into the applications of foods, herbs, and ashes of certain metals that have an enlivening and purifying effect on the body, they were among the world's first alchemists, from which our modern knowledge of medicine and chemistry evolved. A few hundred years ago, European alchemists also endeavored to discover the "elixir" of life.

While material substances can be beneficially used by one who is knowledgeable about their actions and effects, the real vitalizers are the regenerative substances produced in the body when one accomplishes an advanced degree of spiritual realization and formerly dormant soul forces become expressive. Stress management and regular meditation practice also results in a slight reduction of body temperature and provides deep rest to the mind and to all systems of the body. It has been discovered, for instance, that men and women who are of middle-age or older, who meditate regularly, are usually biologically younger than their peers who do not meditate.

Answers to Questions About Reincarnation and the Causes of Personal Circumstances

When inquiring into life's processes to discover why certain events and circumstances occur, the following questions may surface in the mind:

Q. *Do we have to continue to reincarnate until we work out or neutralize all of our karma?*
A. No. There is no cosmic law that determines that all desires and subconscious tendencies and conditionings have to be worked out or expressed. So long as we remain at a level of consciousness which corresponds to our karmic condition, we are likely to be influenced by it. When we awaken to clear states of consciousness, we are removed from karmic conditions related to former states just as one who awakens from a dream is removed from the conditions of the dream state. When our understanding improves, we can renounce self-defeating attitudes, feelings, and behaviors. The superior influences of superconscious states also weaken destructive subconscious tendencies and purify and illumine the mind. Meditators who are very advanced may, upon becoming aware of dormant karmic tendencies, either remove them by intention or let the potency of influential subconscious desires

and tendencies be exhausted during interludes of conscious visions (superconscious dreams). If one is not established in Self-awareness while experiencing visions, there may be a tendency to become overly involved with them. The more direct way to neutralize subconscious tendencies and desires is to acknowledge and discard those which can be discerned and have the remainder of karma weakened and removed by constructive actions and superconscious influences.

Q. *Is it true that children born with birth defects or who die young did something wrong in a previous incarnation and are now reaping the effects of their actions?*
A. No. There can be a variety of causes of birth defects: the genetic characteristics of the parents; inadequate nutrition of the mother; the presence of toxic matters in the mother's system, such as drugs, alcohol, pesticide residues and other poisons from the environment. Whatever can happen to a spiritually unawake soul can be experienced in the physical realm. Attempts to determine specific karmic causes for every human situation are futile. Unless we are enlightened, it is human nature to be inclined to accept answers that will pacify our minds and feelings. When we are in conditioned states of consciousness, we may grasp at almost any explanation that seems to us to be a reasonable answer to our questions or that will provide us a degree of emotional comfort.

Q. *Are people who are either impoverished or prosperous experiencing the effects of their thoughts and actions during a previous incarnation?*
A. Not always. While we can experience the effects of the momentum of intentions, attitudes, tendencies, and

behaviors from one incarnation to another, our present circumstances are usually a reflection of our present states of consciousness, attitudes, and behaviors. By right use of imagination, will, and action, we can overcome limiting circumstances. Some souls are born into conditions of poverty and do not rise above them. Others, in similar conditions, choose to expand their consciousness and learn to be in the flow of the limitless resources of the universe. It is often convenient to blame present conditions on past, unknown causes. The healthy-minded, emotionally mature approach is to be responsible in the present for our spiritual growth and our personal circumstances.

Q. *If one starts on the spiritual path and becomes distracted from it, does it require several incarnations to get back on it?*
A. Time is not an influential factor. All that is required is decisive choice and right endeavor. It is characteristic of people to start a new venture with good intentions and be distracted from it or lose interest. Just as one can temporarily fall away from the spiritual path, so one can become lost in a maze of philosophical concepts and practices that may actually be a diversion from living a goal-directed life. Many presume themselves to be on the spiritual path are but dabbling with various ideas and systems rather than being intent on the ultimate goal of liberation of consciousness.

Q. *Do souls have to be reincarnated in both male and female bodies and have a variety of experiences in order to accomplish well-balanced spiritual development?*
A. Spiritual growth is not directly related to the roles we play or the variety of experiences we have; it is a matter of awakening to Self-knowledge that allows comprehen-

sion and experience of who we are in relationship to the Infinite. While what we do and experience in the mundane realm may sometimes be helpful to our mental and emotional development, the great essential is to awaken from relative circumstances and have awareness restored to wholeness. This accomplished, we no longer have to speculate about future incarnations. We live consciously in the flow of God's grace with purified understanding.

Q. *Do some souls have a karmic relationship or a common destiny that brings them together many times in this and other spheres of the universe?*
A. Yes. Souls with close mental and emotional relationships may, because of their mutual attraction or attachment, meet many times in this and other realms. This does not mean that these relationships are needed, only that they are the result of similar states of consciousness and interests. If such relationships are supportive of one's highest good, they can be continued. If relationships are harmful or interfere with spiritual growth, they can be healed or renounced. More useful, are those relationships which are the result of a common soul destiny, because they are entirely supportive and enable cooperative endeavors. The most useful relationship is that of a devotee of God and the guru (teacher) who demonstrates and reveals the way to soul freedom. When there is close attunement with one's enlightenment path, at the time of transition, highly God-realized souls in subtle realms related to that path can be attracted. They can be present to assist the departing soul to its next level of unfoldment and to complete liberation if the soul is prepared for that final experience.

What Happens When We Die to this World, and How to Depart Consciously at the Right Time

The ideal time to depart this world is after spiritual growth has been accomplished, all duties and obligations are fulfilled, and the body is no longer needed. To desire to leave the body before all of our purposes are fulfilled is irresponsible. If we are "tired of living," we are not living correctly. We have freedom of choice to arrange our circumstances, relationships, and activities so that living is meaningful and enjoyable. We do not have to allow ourselves to become overstressed, worn out, confused, or confined to oppressive conditions. Instead of thinking about having ideal circumstances in the distant future, it is healthier, and more enjoyable, to choose and demonstrate ideal circumstances in the present.

Transition from the body when the time is right is natural and easy. Biological processes slow down, life forces internalize and flow to the brain, and the soul makes its exit. Having fulfilled all major purposes, with no compelling desires or attachments remaining, at the moment of transition one has but to contemplate being free in the Infinite. A shift of viewpoint can then occur that makes possible identification with astral or causal spheres or their transcendence. The easiest way for devotees to accomplish their final exit from the body is to contemplate and awaken to pure consciousness. This may be accomplished instantaneously by an act of intention.

When the time for transition is near, one should meditate, merging in the inner light and sound, contemplating the Absolute. Advanced meditators can consciously leave the body by withdrawing attention from externals, flowing it and their awareness upward through the vital centers in the spine to the spiritual eye and higher brain, and merging awareness in the Om vibration and inner light. The soul and vital forces then consciously exit the body from the higher brain centers. The process of gradual withdrawal can be accomplished by removing attention from externals, then from emotional and mental states, and finally from astral and causal awareness so that only awareness of pure consciousness remains.

If concentration is not steady during transition, if awareness is involved with unstable emotional states and persistent mental activity, there is a possibility that one will leave in a partially confused state similar to that which is experienced when meditating with emotions and thought processes still influential. If aspiration to clear awareness is strong, confusion is soon dispelled after transition. If one gives in to fluctuating emotional states and random thought processes, there is a possibility of remaining confused and experiencing dreamlike astral episodes for an extended duration, followed by either emerging into a more clear state or being reincarnated in a new physical body. When dying to this world, it is best to focus on the brilliant, white light that is inwardly revealed and aspire to pure consciousness, avoiding involvement with emotional states, memories, and mental imagery.

One who is consciously undergoing the transition process should be allowed to be quiet and secluded so that concentration is undisturbed. If one is less conscious, tired, or in need of support at the time of transition, a spiritually conscious friend or assistant can sit quietly nearby and meditate in silence. If agreeable to the person who needs support while undergoing transition, quiet chanting of Om, or audible reading of appropriate verses of scripture can be provided until transition has been completed. Family members or others who are emotionally upset should be excluded.

Before the time of transition, one should put in writing their wishes for the disposition of their remaining personal possessions and of their body. A legal will should be prepared, properly witnessed and signed, and placed in a secure place where it can be obtained by family members or by someone who will be responsible for fulfilling the wishes of the deceased. It can also be helpful to put in writing one's wishes regarding the use of life-support procedures in the event this decision has to be made by someone else. Attending to these matters is an indication of emotional maturity and acknowledgment of one's physical mortality. Just as we should be responsible for how we live while on earth, so we should be responsible for efficiently concluding our visit here.

Cremation is the most convenient way to dispose of the body. After being subjected to extreme temperatures for a few hours the body is completely vaporized, its elements released into the atmosphere, leaving only approximately seven pounds of bone fragments for the average adult body. These are then pulverized and may be disposed of however one has decided. Cremation immediately releases the elements of the body into the field of nature, is efficient, and is less costly than burial or entombment of the body in a mausoleum.

Upon leaving the body, the individualized spirit, with its life forces, continues its experiences in astral or causal realms as determined by its state of consciousness or desires. If sufficiently Self-realized, it transcends all manifested realms and awareness is returned to the Field of Pure Consciousness. Family members and friends should not grieve over or worry about the departed soul. Nor should they endeavor to communicate with it. It has left this world, has completed its purpose for being here, and is continuing its awakening in God. Those who had a close relationship may wish to convene a quiet, meditative memorial service for the purpose of coming to terms with their sense of loss and to pray for the welfare of the soul which is now released into the Infinite.

All of us come into the physical realm to sojourn for but a brief duration. We come from inner space and to inner space we are destined to return. No one can prevent this process. It should be comprehended and accepted without regret or attachments of any kind.

Living Free, in Tune with the Infinite, Can be Experienced in this Incarnation

It is a wise devotee of God who forsakes the hope of future soul freedom in favor of choosing to demonstrate it now. Because at our innermost level of being we are ever whole and perfect, our innate wholeness and perfection can be expressed to the degree that we allow it to be actualized. A major soul-inhibiting characteristic of many devotees is conscious or unconscious denial of their divinity. They may aspire to Self-realization. They may endeavor to conform to behaviors which they believe to be necessary to prove their dedication. Yet, in spite of their aspiration and their actions, they do not believe it is possible for them to accomplish spiritual growth. They allow their awareness to be conflicted by remaining attached to their conditioned habits, routine relationships, clouded states of consciousness, programmed mental states, moods, and conditioned reactions to events that occur in their lives. They rationalize their "human condition," make excuses for being inept or undisciplined, and tend to blame karma, planetary influences, or circumstances believed to be beyond their control. They may tend to cling to a belief system that is not valid, not clearly discern the reality of God and their own true nature, or forever look to something or someone outside of themselves for assurance of their salvation.

A spiritual aspirant should have complete faith in God and in causative principles that can result in complete psychological transformation and spiritual growth. The results of such actions will be a blossoming of innate qualities, the ability to wisely use creative powers, orderly unfoldments of circumstances that provide them security and well-being, and increasing evidence of the influences of God's grace in their lives. A dedicated devotee should live as though enlightened, by adhering to the lifestyle and spiritual practice guidelines recommended by God-realized teachers. This should be done, not because doing so creates good karma, but because living like this is the ideal way to live.

Any reasonably intelligent person who is not yet enlightened can choose to live more freely than they habitually do. The alternative is unpleasant and painful: it is to be a victim of circumstances or passively hope and aimlessly strive for improvement with little or no possibility for successful accomplishment.

Our highest good is available to us now. Knowing this, we should immediately and joyously accept it.

Five

Awakening Through the Stages of Spiritual Growth

Souls are destined to awaken from the dream of mortality to full realization of God. There are seven discernible stages through which souls progress from ignorance of the truth about themselves to illumination of consciousness. The most effective way to make soul unfoldment easier is to renounce characteristics which restrict it, while intentionally cultivating mental attitudes, states of consciousness, and behaviors which are characteristic of more conscious levels. Sincere aspiration to spiritual growth, knowledgeable personal endeavor, and responsiveness to the soul's innate urge to have awareness restored to wholeness make growth easier and more rapid.

1. *Unconsciousness.* At this stage, awareness is so completely identified with the physical body and mental processes that the soul mistakenly presumes itself to be a body-mind being only. Mental dullness, apathy, boredom, and provincialism or narrow-mindedness are common characteristics. Spiritual awareness is lacking and intellectual powers are minimal. If one is religious, prayer is usually directed to an imagined form or aspect of God. Activities and relationships are ordinary, as necessary for survival or as one is inclined by desires or whims. Memories, habits, learned or acquired behaviors, and social and cultural influences tend to determine one's lifestyle.

2. *Dysfunctional self-consciousness.* Mental confusion, irrational thinking, and conflicted emotional states are characteristics at this stage. Egocentric identification with the personality-self prevails. Meditation and other spiritual practices may be used in the hope that a degree of inner peace may result. One may believe in angels, be attracted to magic or sorcery, or practice mediumship or "channeling" in a misguided endeavor to communicate with souls in astral realms or with beings in other dimensions who are presumed to have superior knowledge and powers. Powers of intellectual discrimination are weak. Illusions, addictions, sensual desires, dependent emotional relationships, self-defeating behaviors, neurotic needs, complaints, faultfinding, and fantasies about everyday matters and higher realities are common. Emotions and subconscious conditionings tend to determine thoughts and behaviors.

3. *Functional self-consciousness.* A more superior, healthy-minded, yet still egocentric human condition. Rational, nurturing choices usually determine behaviors and relationships. Goal-oriented actions are routinely performed with reasonable skill. Partial intellectual understanding of the reality of God may be present, mixed with traditional or superstitious beliefs. One may be more interested in accessing divine influences to acquire powers or for improving personal circumstances than in Self-discovery and God-realization. Meditation and prayer may be focused on physical and psychological well-being or used to improve abilities to accomplish personal goals. While spiritual growth may be desired, one tends to be more interested in and involved with mundane projects.

4. *Superconsciousness.* Superconscious states are experienced when transformations of awareness are refined and subdued, allowing clear perceptions of one's true nature, God, and transcendent realities. The sense of independent selfhood diminishes with increasing Self-realization. Activities and relationships are wisely chosen and experienced without compulsion. Aspiration to liberation of consciousness is sincere and compelling. One at this stage of soul unfoldment can be a devoted and competent disciple (learner) on the spiritual path.

5. *Cosmic Consciousness.* As superconscious states become influential and self-consciousness diminishes, apprehension of the universe as a play of cosmic forces emanating from God's being improves. When meditating, perceptions and realizations are transcendent and one comprehends the universe to be a manifestation of primordial nature: Om, cosmic particles, space, and time. Activities and relationships are enjoyed with higher understanding. Soul capacities increase to allow improved comprehension and more vivid experience of the reality of God. Ignorance, selfishness, and indifference about the welfare of others cease as the soul qualities of innate knowledge, selflessness, and compassion unfold. Soul abilities become pronounced and are wisely demonstrated.

6. *God-Consciousness.* Realization of God. If mental conditionings (karmic impressions) remain, their influences are weakened and finally removed. Selfless, insightful actions prevent the accumulation of further mental conditionings. As God-consciousness increases, the soul is liberated from delusions and attachments.

7. *Full Enlightenment.* Complete knowledge of God and of cosmic processes; the fully awake state. When relating to mundane realms, enlightenment is undiminished and all actions are spontaneously appropriate. Ego-sense remains only as a viewpoint from which to observe subjective realities and objective circumstances without restricting God-realization.

We can awaken quickly through these stages by aspiring to ever higher levels of understanding and applying new knowledge until we have validated it by personal experience. By this practical means, we can skillfully and enjoyably progress from the seeker-of-truth stage to being a conscious, fully functional knower of the truth about ourselves and our relationship with the Infinite.

> Considering pleasure and displeasure, gain and loss, victory and defeat with even-mindedness, engage in right endeavor. Thus you shall not incur misfortune. This is the wisdom of the ancient seers. Now hear it. Apply it by dedicated practice. With this knowledge you shall remove yourself from the laws of mundane causation. By this right way no endeavor is wasted and no obstacle prevails. — *Bhagavad Gita 2:38-40*

Six

How to Live With Meaningful Purpose

Are we living every moment with a clear sense of purpose? Are all of our purposes meaningful (of real value)? If we are even mildly curious about the many opportunities life provides for observation and experience, it is not difficult to be attracted to something of interest and to devote our time, energies, and resources to a variety of activities and relationships. The question we need to ask is: When I have completed my projects, satisfied my desires, and fulfilled my commitments, will all my actions have been worthwhile?

A life which is not effectively lived with clear knowledge of meaningful purpose is almost entirely wasted. Although a few lessons may be learned, some skills may be acquired, and a degree of spiritual growth may naturally occur, opportunities to awaken to illumination of consciousness, the primary purpose for our having been born into the natural world, are neglected and the soul's innate urge to be free is frustrated.

When we know how to live, are sustained by faith, and motivated and energized by a Self-confident will to excel, we can redeem the troubled past, live efficiently, and be assured of continuous unfoldments of good fortune.

Confidence grounded in Self-knowledge is superior to personality-based self-esteem which often needs constant reassurance and may falter in the face of challenge, when we are tired, or when circumstances are not satisfying. When we are Self-knowledgeably confident it is easy to be enthusiastic, enjoyable to envision desired outcomes of plans and actions, rewarding to see through appearances of discord to harmonious possibilities that can be actualized, pleasant to accept good fortune that is immediately available, and natural to have our highest good come into manifestation by our concentrated intention, unwavering faith, and effective actions.

Confidence grounded in Self-knowledge can only prevail when the ego is purified. Deluded awareness is the illusory sense of believing ourselves to be independent of God. When we mistakenly believe that we are other than an individualized expression of God's consciousness, we are subject to further confusion, paranoia, loneliness, and fear. For one who is knowledgable, the idea, cherished by many in conditioned states of consciousness, that the ego needs to be protected, nurtured, and preserved, is known to be foolishness. The ego is purified by insightful analysis of our core essence, renunciation of self-centeredness in favor of Self-knowledge, nurturing awareness of the presence of God, and regular episodes of superconscious meditation that culminate in transcendent realizations.

We can discover the best way to live by determining how to most effectively use our talents and abilities, being curious about and envisioning possibilities, engaging in endeavors which are soul-satisfying, praying for guidance, and being receptive and responsive to worthwhile circumstances, events, and relationships which are presented to us. We need not ask anyone what they think we should do; we can rely on our own common sense, intuitive guidance, personal initiative, and the intelligently directed Power that nurtures and enlivens the universe and us. To know whether or not we are on the right course, we have only to examine our mental and emotional states, the depth of our soul peace, and the results of our endeavors. If our thoughts are habitually orderly and rational, if we are always optimistic, happy, emotionally content, soul-centered, and satisfied with the results of our endeavors, we are on the right course.

To live effectively and be spiritually fulfilled we need to be aware of the following four primary aims of life and successfully accomplish them.

Live in Tune with the Infinite and Have a Harmonious Relationship with the Universe (1)

Our attunement with the Infinite is experienced and a responsive relationship is established with it by expanding awareness to become more God-conscious and by discovering how we can best function in the world in accord with our understanding, skills, and creative abilities. We are then able to learn, grow, and successfully function with the full support of nature's evolutionary influences and God's grace.

Cosmic influences and actions which uphold and maintain the universe and its processes originate with the impulse of the Oversoul aspect of God to express, resulting in evolutionary processes which contribute to orderly transformation and unfoldment. Personal behaviors which support and maintain our lives are those which are appropriate to our needs for well-being and spiritual growth in accord with nature's laws. In various religious scriptures, this way of living is referred to as "the way of righteousness." By living up to our full potential, we make a useful contribution to society and to nature and are nurtured and sustained by the universe and God's grace. As we become more conscious and our skills improve, we learn by experience, observation, and revelation how to live effectively.

Very few souls are born into this world with clear awareness of their true nature or are conscious of why they came here. Soul awareness, clouded by subconscious memories and unconscious tendencies accumulated through many incarnations in this and other realms, is more commonly identified with the infant body and the circumstances of its new environment. Because of the deluded soul's dependent condition, its inclination is to adapt behaviors which will enable it to survive and relate to others.

Many souls complete their life cycle on earth without awakening to Self-knowledge or seriously thinking about why they are here. They either do not experience spontaneous spiritual awakening that expands awareness and enables them to view themselves and their circumstances in a new way, or they remain self-centeredly preoccupied with narrow interests, routine endeavors, and emotionally dependent relationships. While they may have the capacity to grow and learn, they may not aspire to do so, or they may choose to remain "only human" in order to appear normal to family members, friends, neighbors, or business associates. If we are sincerely intent upon unfolding and expressing our spiritual potential, we can relate appropriately to others when necessary without compromising our principles or neglecting matters which are important to our well-being and the fulfillment of our meaningful purposes.

Even for more aware souls, several years of growing through the stages of childhood and young adulthood, which is sometimes pleasant and sometimes painful and frustrating, may be experienced before Self-awareness blossoms and knowledge about their purpose for being here becomes defined. If aspiration to spiritual growth and fulfillment of meaningful purposes is pronounced, one may immediately embrace learning and growing opportunities with enthusiasm. If aspiration is feeble, addictive tendencies are strong, powers of intelligence are weak, or Self-confidence and courage are lacking, one may be inclined to remain habit-bound, be unable or unwilling to exercise discernment, be confused, or be afraid to implement constructive changes in behaviors and lifestyle.

To have the support of the universe, we need both lower and higher knowledge: practical knowledge about the world that enables us to live effectively, and insightful knowledge of ourselves as spiritual beings, of God, and of how subtle spiritual and mental causes produce corresponding effects. While our faith and God's grace can be supportive of us when our vision of possibilities is unclear and we are unable to help ourselves, we should banish any tendency to be intellectually or physically lazy or to nurture erroneous beliefs and illusions. To be accomplished, live effectively, and be spiritually enlightened, we need to directly confront and clearly comprehend the reality of life. Because the possibilities for acquiring useful knowledge to enable us to function more effectively and experience unfoldments of Self-revealed knowledge that liberates the spirit are almost limitless, our secular and metaphysical education should continue for the duration of our sojourn in time and space. To be satisfied with partial understanding and incomplete spiritual growth is to prefer continued bondage to ignorance instead of the complete freedom that can be ours by choice, concentrated endeavor, and God's grace.

Some souls, having already awakened to advanced levels of spiritual awareness soon after coming into the world, become aware that they have a specific mission to fulfill that will be of benefit to society and be instrumental in facilitating the spiritual awakening of others. They have either chosen to do this work or, because of their knowledge, skills, and responsiveness, are willing agents of evolutionary impulses which support and transform nature and contribute to the awakening of others. While rendering helpful service, they can continue to awaken to complete Self-knowledge and God-realization.

Even if we do not have clear conviction of a mission-purpose, when aspiration to spiritual growth is compelling and commitment to it is unwavering, progress is easier and more rapid when we choose a wisdom-guided life-path. Doing this will naturally result in ego purification, psychological transformation, unfoldment and actualization of spiritual qualities, responsible self-care and service-oriented behavior instead of self-centered acquisitiveness (compelling desire to gain or possess something motivated by insecurity or greed), a harmonious relationship with all aspects of nature, and an abundance of evidence of God's grace.

Our daily interlude of prayer and meditation requires but a portion of a twenty-four hour day. During most of our waking hours we are engaged in thinking, working, the performance of routine duties, and relationships. Living wholesomely, constructively, and appropriately with conscious intention is the most effective spiritual practice available to us. Anyone who asserts that the performance of duties and the fulfillment of obligations does not allow time for spiritual practice, either does not know that right living *is* spiritual practice or is offering a weak excuse for their disinterest and lack of self-discipline.

Any work we do, service we render, or action we perform that produces entirely constructive results, is life-enhancing. It is beneficial to us and benefits all who are in any way affected by it. When we are attentive and disciplined, only constructive impulses, thoughts, and desires will emerge in the mind. Our speech will be constructive. Our emotional states will be regulated and positive. Integrity and compassion will determine our behaviors. We will be established in Self-knowledge, ever aware of our relationship with the Infinite. We will consciously live with meaningful purpose.

Have Life-Enhancing Desires Easily Fulfilled (2)

Having our life-enhancing desires easily fulfilled allows us to live with enjoyment and frees attention to enable us to accomplish purposes without worry or strain. Life-enhancing desires are wholesome and entirely beneficial when fulfilled. Desires essential to our survival and well-being and which make possible the accomplishment of worthwhile endeavors need not interfere with our spiritual growth. The desires to renounce are those driven by restlessness, unwholesome or immoral cravings, addictive tendencies, and self-centered whims and inclinations. If allowed to dominate thoughts and behaviors, they cause psychological conflicts, weaken the body's immune system, suppress soul qualities, contract awareness, and interfere with endeavors to live effectively and supportively relate to others.

Desires have the potency to cause effects by their influential force and by attracting circumstances which correspond to them. Passionate, willful desire serves only the ego and usually results in unhappiness and misfortune. For one who aspires to spiritual growth, more productive of beneficial results than forceful desire is gentle intention arising from soul awareness, nurtured by faith in the certainty of the outcome. When something is wanted or needed, our soul-felt conviction that we already have it is causative. It clears our awareness, enables us to perceive available opportunities and possibilities, energizes the mind, awakens creative forces in the body, motivates us to appropriate actions when actions are necessary, and influences the universe to be favorably responsive.

As spiritual beings, one of the several abilities we have when we are Self-aware is that of having our desires spontaneously fulfilled by pure intention. When desires are clearly defined and faith is not disturbed by doubt, their fulfillment is the natural outcome. If we desire supportive circumstances, healing of any kind, improved mental powers, or spiritual awakening and unfoldment, we have only to sincerely want these results and accept them at the deepest level of our being and they will soon be experienced. If we can do something to assist ourselves to fulfillment, we should do it. If we do not know what to do, we can acquire helpful knowledge. As our faith remains unwavering, subtle influences of mind and consciousness can produce the desired results. If we do not have a clearly defined mental concept of ideal circumstances, we can intend, believe, and expect our highest good to quickly unfold, and it will.

We can also desire the highest good for others and, with faith, release that desire into Universal Mind. When doing this, there should be no attempt to control or manipulate them or their circumstances to conform to what we might think is best for them. When others who are interested in learning how to experience their highest good ask us for help, we can inform them of the principles that determine effective living and how to apply them, encourage them in their endeavors, and provide for them the example of our own rational, enlightened behavior.

Be Affluent: Always in the Flow of Resources and Supportive Events and Circumstances (3)

When our relationship with the universe is harmonious, we are included in its processes and it provides our needs. Flows of resources, relationships, circumstances, and events which contribute to our highest good are spontaneous and continuous. We are assured of being always prosperous: thriving, flourishing, and being successful.

The universe, as a manifestation of cosmic forces emanated from the Godhead, is self-complete, self-referring, and self-repairing. It's energy is constant, subject to being transformed while neither increasing nor decreasing. Because the universe is a manifestation of God's consciousness and cosmic forces, when our comprehension is clear and we trust implicitly in God's grace and the actions of the universe, we need not experience lack or limitation of any kind. If we do, it is not that resources are unavailable; we only need to be more Self-knowledgeable and improve our understanding of and relationship with the reality of God and with universal forces.

We can have whatever we need by enlarging our capacity to acknowledge and accept it. This is accomplished by replacing feelings of unworthiness, pessimism, poverty ideas, self-centered personal behaviors, addictive or destructive relationships, and mood-impelled, vaguely performed actions with convictions of Self-worth, optimism, prosperity ideas, soul-directed personal behaviors, wholesome relationships, and intentional, purposeful actions. Sitting to meditate every day is the immediate way to remove awareness from personality-based limitations and experience pure consciousness. Resting in this clear state, we can remind ourselves that out of our awareness of what we are, our objective experiences unfold. When we are permanently established in Self-knowledge and vividly aware of our relationship with God, it is easy to discard characteristics of the self-conscious condition and freely live with insightful understanding.

To be affluent, in the flow of resources and circumstances which are entirely supportive of us, we need to be willing to participate with life's processes. We need to give of ourselves, generously share our knowledge and available resources, and be service-oriented agents of the Higher Power that sustains the forces of evolution and impels the awakening and spiritual unfoldment of souls. To think that by giving we will receive is to remain self-centered and limited. To know that by right giving of ourselves and of available resources we remain in the flow of good fortune, is the way of higher knowledge and is prospering. All that God is, we can know and experience. The reality of God extends to all planes and realms of universal manifestation. Where we are, everything we need already exists or can be manifested.

There is nothing we can do to diminish or increase the everywhere present reality of God. When God's presence is not obviously experienced, we need only to improve our powers of perception. We can look at the world scene to be reminded that what we see was produced by God. We can calm thoughts by prayer and introspective meditation to become aware of ourselves as individualized units of God's consciousness. For a reasonably aware person, the existence of God cannot be denied because of the overwhelming outer evidence of the senses, the inner testimony of intuitive knowing, and the occasions—whether fleeting or lingering—of personal vivid experience. God's reality includes invisible, omnipresent consciousness, the energies that form and animate the cosmos, the elements and substance of nature, and the trillions of souls that inhabit fine, subtle, and gross realms.

Experience Rapid, Progressive, Authentic Spiritual Growth that Culminates in Mental Illumination and Spiritual Enlightenment (4)

Spiritual growth is rapid and progressive when we focus on essentials and eliminate nonessentials. It is authentic when knowledge and expanded states of awareness can be demonstrated easily in practical ways.

Because we are spiritual beings, we cannot be completely satisfied only to have a harmonious relationship with the universe, have desires easily fulfilled, and have resources and circumstances spontaneously available to meet our needs and to accomplish our mundane purposes. Although these accomplishments can make our lives more satisfying and free us to explore transcendent possibilities, to be completely fulfilled there is something else we need to accomplish. While learning to live effectively, we need to direct our attention and endeavors to awakening and unfolding our innate soul qualities and capacities to their full extent. We need to rid the mind of confusion, nurture spiritual growth, and be established in Self-knowledge and God-realization.

The ideal way to demonstrate commitment to the enlightenment path is to daily attend to spiritual practices before directing attention to mundane matters. Doing this floods the mind and body with superconscious influences, refines the nervous system, awakens and circulates regenerative energies, produces mental and emotional stability, enables us to think rationally and make intelligent decisions, neutralizes compulsive tendencies and urges, and attunes us to the Infinite Life. Our ideal should be to live effectively in the world while remaining untouched by and unattached to it. Regular interludes of contemplative meditation and quiet reflection provide us the understanding and inner poise to do this.

Because our innate urge is to have our awareness restored to wholeness, when we eliminate all restrictions to this inclination, spiritual growth occurs spontaneously. When we deny our innate urge to be God-realized, when we prefer ignorance to wisdom, self-consciousness to Self-knowledge, and egocentric attitudes and behaviors to expansion of awareness and life-enhancing behaviors, we remain in self-chosen bondage. Regardless of our personal or environmental circumstances, we can choose to awaken from all limiting conditions.

Our role in the spiritual growth process is to aspire to it, renounce delusions and illusions, and do what we can to prepare our mind and body to allow free flows of soul awareness. As we progress on the awakening path, we discover that we are assisted to fulfillment by the impulses of God's grace. Resolved to be God-realized and prepared by right endeavor, we have only to yield to the purifying, transformative actions of grace that emerge from within the depths of our being.

> I thought that my voyage had come to its end, that the path before me was closed, that provisions were exhausted and the time had come to take shelter in a silent obscurity. But I find that Thy will knows no end in me, and when old words die out on the tongue, new melodies break forth from the heart, and where the old tracks are lost, new country is revealed in its wonders.
>
> — *Rabindranath Tagore*

Seven

The Higher Knowledge and Transformative Actions That Restore Soul Awareness to Wholeness

To restore our awareness to its original, whole status we need to be able to discern the difference between our real, permanent pure conscious nature and the fragmented states of ordinary awareness commonly experienced when our attention is overly identified with thoughts, memories, emotional states, and sensory perceptions. We can then skillfully engage in constructive actions that result in Self-discovery and enlightenment.

Consciousness is what we are; awareness always involves an object. We are aware, as a witness or observer, of our thoughts, feelings, moods, perceptions, and environment. We may sometimes inappropriately use the words *awareness* and *consciousness*. For instance, we may say, "I am conscious of my circumstances," instead of, "I am aware of my circumstances." Because we may not always clearly define the words we use, we may not know what it means to be truly conscious. Although our awareness may be conflicted and clouded; we, as individualized units of God's consciousness, remain ever pure.

For undiscerning people, because the distinction between themselves as conscious beings and ordinary awareness is clouded, suffering results. They tend to identify with fragmented states of awareness and mistakenly presume that they are fated to be victims of their present circumstances. To be enlightened, we must be removed from ordinary states of awareness so that our essential nature can be revealed as the foundation of freedom distinct from ordinary conflicted and clouded states of awareness. Accomplishing this is the whole purpose of spiritual inquiry and endeavor. Awakening to realization of it is an ever-present possibility that should be acknowledged rather than thought of as a hoped-for, distant-future event toward which to aspire.

The persistent transformations which occur in the average person's awareness include (1) mental processing of information; (2) illusions, or incorrect knowing; (3) symbolic ideas, sometimes with fantasies or hallucinations; (4) memories of all kinds; (5) the characteristics of dreaming and sleep (defined as a modification of powers of cognition or knowing). These obstacles can be transcended by removing attention from them or they can be subdued so that pure consciousness alone remains.

If transformations of awareness are temporarily transcended, insight may enable one to more easily relate to and regulate mental and emotional states after the interlude of transcendence. Even if transformations of awareness are made dormant to the extent that a degree of mental peace is experienced during the waking state or during sleep, this can be helpful because the nervous system is provided some rest, stress is reduced, and energies can be renewed. The ideal, whether removing attention from restless thoughts and emotional states by transcending them or by making them temporarily dormant, is to experience clear awareness and pure states of consciousness. To attempt to ignore mental transformations or to temporarily suppress them while remaining self-conscious or ego-fixated will not result in noticeable improvement of psychological states or of personal circumstances.

If immediate awakening to transcendence is not possible, an intentional way to allow the emergence of pure consciousness is to recognize and subdue or eliminate inclinations common to the ordinary human condition. These are (1) to confuse the difference between pure consciousness and ordinary states of awareness; (2) to identify with ego-awareness, the false sense of individuality; (3) to be attached to pleasant experiences; (4) to be overly concerned about the possibility of having painful experiences; (5) to be preoccupied with fear of death, which may be instinctive or due to latent memories of past episodes of dying. The following characteristics are common to the deluded condition: (1) lack of knowledge of the true nature of the Self; (2) ego identification; (3) thinking and perceptual errors; (4) tenacious attachment to fixed ideas and objective circumstances.

Various methods and techniques for resisting, restraining, weakening, making dormant, and removing the characteristics of ordinary awareness which obscure pure consciousness may be applied and practiced with benefit. These may include (1) disciplined endeavor to regulate them; (2) cultivation of dispassion and renunciation (non-attachment); (3) meditation that provides repeated superconscious experience and allows pure consciousness to be unveiled; (4) various supplemental practices.

Supplemental practices according to one's psychological temperament, personal capacity, and need may include (1) nurturing of faith along with persistence in intentional endeavors which are known to be useful; (2) the cultivation of devotion to God or to the ideal of enlightenment; (3) enhancement of intellectual and intuitive powers and Self-awareness; (4) routines and regimens to improve health and increase vitality. It can also be supportive to study scriptures and other sources to acquire helpful information for inspiration and to confirm personal insights and psychological and spiritual growth experiences. For centuries, these basic practices have been taught by teachers of various enlightenment traditions because their usefulness has been verified by personal experimentation. They are but the means of accomplishment. They fall away or can be discarded when permanent enlightenment results in actions which are always appropriate.

Awareness of ourselves as beings of pure consciousness, and spontaneous spiritual growth, results in beneficial changes in mental attitude, knowledge of Self-worth and inclinations to naturally choose compassionate and purposeful lifestyle behaviors. For overall improvement in well-being and faster spiritual growth, it is recommended that one choose to live wholesomely and perform only constructive actions.

For harmonious relationships and psychological health, and to weaken and eliminate troublesome mental conditionings and unregulated transformations which fragment and cloud awareness, five external disciplines are to be perfected: (1) harmlessness; (2) truthfulness; (3) honesty; (4) conservation and transmutation of vital forces by mastery of attention and actions; (5) responsible, nonpossessive behaviors.

Harmlessness is perfected when actions are supportive and life-enhancing and when inclinations to injure others, ourselves, living things, or the environment are absent. We then live on friendly terms with a friendly universe.

Truthfulness is perfected when we are spiritually aware and in tune with the infinite. Our thoughts, feelings, and actions are then integrated and impulses of constructive desires cause immediate, corresponding effects. Devoid of mental confusion and emotional conflict, our intentions easily manifest with the cooperation of nature's laws and resources.

Honesty is perfected when thoughts and behaviors are righteous: when they are moral, ethical, and appropriate. Honesty is essential for prosperity.

Mastery of attention is necessary for rational thinking, purposeful living, focused concentration, successful meditation practice, and for discerning the difference between pure consciousness and ordinary, confused states of awareness. Mastery of actions allows effective living.

Conservation and transmutation of vital forces is accomplished by avoiding thoughts, feelings, and behaviors which waste them while choosing thoughts, feelings, and behaviors which enhance them. Irrational thinking, worry, anxiety, emotional conflicts, excessive talking, compulsiveness, restlessness, purposeless actions, dissipation of all kinds, misuse of or addiction to chemical substances or food, insufficient sleep, excessive use of the senses, laziness, poor health habits, and all other behaviors that weaken or deplete vital forces should be renounced. Conservation of vital forces results in mental clarity, improved powers of concentration, radiant health, and more rapid spiritual growth. Conserved vital forces energize the mind, strengthen the body's immune system, enliven the cerebrospinal centers, nourish the brain, and improve powers of concentration and meditation practice.

Responsible, nonpossesive behaviors are natural to us when our awareness is expanded, we know how to live effectively, and soul qualities of compassion and generosity are allowed free expression. Irresponsible, self-serving behaviors are common to people who are egocentric, fearful, and uncharitable. It is our moral and spiritual duty to do what is necessary for our well-being and the well-being of others with whom we are in relationship, and it is acceptable for us to have and use things and resources which are available to us in this world. Obsessive attachments confine soul awareness and restrict the unfoldment of innate qualities and capacities. Egocentric attitudes and behaviors prevent spiritual growth.

The five internal disciplines to be perfected are (1) purity of thoughts and motives; (2) inner contentment in all circumstances; (3) psychological transformation by insightful analysis and elimination of harmful psychological characteristics, addictive tendencies, self-defeating attitudes and habits, delusions, illusions, and irrational or emotional response when painful experiences are remembered; (4) meditation practice; (5) surrender of self-conscious states of awareness to allow Self-knowledge and God-realization to unfold and be actualized.

Purity of thoughts and motives should always determine our choices of environment, lifestyle, diet, relationships, work, and habitual behaviors. When our thoughts and motives are pure, everything we do is supportive of psychological and physical health, ideal circumstances, wholesome relationships, and spiritual growth. The mind cannot be contaminated by anything we might hear or see and our experience of being cannot be disturbed. All of our aspirations and actions are life-enhancing and awareness-expanding.

Soul contentment in all circumstances is perfected when we are established in Self-knowledge and dispassionately disposed toward relationships and circumstances. It confers peace of mind and serene happiness.

Psychological transformation eliminates destructive mental and emotional characteristics. Addictive tendencies are the result of emotional immaturity and mental, emotional, and physical dependency. They can be eliminated by cultivating responsible mental attitudes and personal behaviors. Self-defeating attitudes and habits are rooted in a negative personality self-image, thoughts and feelings of unworthiness, and perhaps a conscious or unconscious desire to withdraw from life, to succumb to circumstances, or die. They can be eliminated by right Self-understanding, acceptance of the fact that we are meant to thrive and be successful, and by nurturing a will to live, creatively express, and grow spiritually. Memories of painful experiences—mistreatment, neglect, rejection, impoverished or limiting circumstances, failure, sickness, accidents, mistakes in judgment, inappropriate personal behavior, and other circumstances or events which when remembered cause an irrational or emotional response—can restrict psychological and spiritual growth. They blur perceptions, weaken powers of concentration and discernment, restrict creative actions, distract and confine attention, contract awareness, impair mental abilities, overstress the nervous system, weaken the body's immune system, diminish energy, and can contribute to dysfunctional neurotic or psychotic behaviors.

We need not be mentally or emotionally disturbed by memories of painful incidents. Because they are only mental impressions of prior events and experiences, they can be dispassionately recalled and viewed, freeing attention, energies, and abilities for meaningful purposes. To allow emotional maturity and unfoldment of soul qualities to be actualized, the life-diminishing habit of neurotic preoccupation with memories of any kind should immediately be renounced.

Erroneous ideas and beliefs can be discarded when they are recognized and by being willing to learn what is true. Lack of spiritual awareness, the primary cause of the delusion that we are helpless, material, mortal creatures can be corrected by acquiring accurate information about God, souls, and the processes of cosmic manifestation, and by aspiring to and nurturing authentic spiritual growth. When we clearly discern the difference between ourselves as beings of pure consciousness and ordinary, afflicted states of awareness, delusions vanish.

Illusions, misperceptions of ideas or of what is perceived, cease when we learn to accurately discern the facts of what is thought about, observed, or experienced. Spiritually unawake people often admit to enjoying their illusions, preferring to remain ignorant of the facts of life because of mental, emotional, or physical complacency, or intellectual laziness.

Regular, focused meditation practice along with supportive supplemental practices contribute to progressive unfoldments of superconscious perceptions and experiences, refined superconscious states, Self-knowledge, and God-realization.

Surrender of self-conscious (egocentric) states for the

purpose of comprehending and experiencing the reality of God is the immediate way to illumination of consciousness. When meditating, after preliminary practice has resulted in mental calm and internalized attention, discard awareness of independent self-sense to acknowledge oneness or wholeness. When not meditating, be mindful of the fact that self-sense is but a viewpoint for perceiving the objective world and that the core nature, pure consciousness, remains ever the same.

Because it is almost impossible for the average person to control mental and emotional states and behaviors by will power, meditation practice is recommended for the purpose of quieting the mind and calming the emotions so that clear states of awareness can be experienced. So long as awareness is afflicted by unregulated mental transformations and constantly changing emotional states, it may be difficult to remove attention from these conditions and experience pure consciousness even with the best of intentions. During alert, focused meditation practice, physical relaxation contributes to emotional calm and mental quietude, breathing becomes slow and refined, body temperature is somewhat reduced, flows of vital forces become harmonized, and concentration is easier.

The cultivation of the recommended external and internal disciplines and regular practice of meditation that results in physical relaxation and mental and emotional peace, are preliminary procedures that restrain the fluctuations and transformations that ordinarily occur in the average person's field of awareness. It is then possible to discern the difference between pure consciousness and states of fragmented awareness and to clearly apprehend (1) the nature of physical existence; (2) the nature of subtle, mental states; (3) how the sensory capacities function; (4) the nature of ordinary, fragmented awareness. These four categories of higher knowledge may be apprehended as the result of patient, intentional, meditative contemplation; gradual, progressive awakenings; or sudden, unexpected unfoldments of Self-revealed knowledge during meditation or at any other time.

The physical manifestation of the universe is the result of God's emanational inclinations and cosmic forces which express the constituent components of primordial nature and regulate their processes. The characteristics of physical existence can be partially comprehended by intellectual analysis; Self-revealed knowledge, provides complete comprehension. When insight dawns, it may seem to us that we are but "remembering" what we once knew before we assumed ego-awareness and became unconsciously involved with mind and matter.

Subtle mental states include impulses empowered by restlessness, impulses because of urges to express, inclinations to satisfy needs, desires of various kinds, addictive inclinations, habits, unconscious and subconscious thought processes, memories, and the multitudinous transformations that tend to constantly occur. The mind processes information. It and its contents are also influenced by the three constituent qualities (*gunas*) that pervade all of nature with their elevating and purifying, inertial, and transformative influences. For awareness to be restored to wholeness, it must be removed from involvement with mental states and from the influences of the qualities of nature. When mental states and the influential qualities of nature are apprehended, it is easier to observe their actions with detachment and either regulate or withdraw attention from them.

The functions of sensory capacities can be apprehended by knowing their origins and how they are produced, and by calm analysis of the processes of smelling, touching, tasting, seeing, and hearing. When our awareness expands, perceptions need not always be confined to the senses; intuitive or extrasensory perception enlarges our capacity to perceive. During meditation, when attention is withdrawn from the senses and directed back to the mind and higher brain centers, we become oblivious of external circumstances. Mental processes, no longer stimulated by sensory perceptions, become refined and calm, allowing intellectual and meditative contemplation to be practiced without distractions.

Ordinary, fragmented awareness causes us to erroneously presume that our consciousness and the universe are other than whole. When our awareness is no longer disturbed and confused by mental transformations, wholeness is directly apprehended.

An experience of pure consciousness mixed with ego identification is supported by awareness of *having* the experience rather than of *being* pure consciousness. When awareness is removed from ego-identification, only pure consciousness remains. When permanently established in Self-knowledge, the soul can consciously express through the purified ego. Mental, emotional, and physical conditions and the influences and actions of nature then no longer cloud the soul's awareness or obscure perceptions. Final liberation, characterized by spontaneous and continuous apprehension of what is true, whether one is meditating or is relating to subjective mental states or to objective circumstances, does not require the support of anything external. This state is referred to as isolation because pure consciousness is permanently removed from the possibility of again being blindly identified with mental states and matter. Having permanently awakened to this unrestricted state, one is enabled to think rationally and to relate to the world with flawless understanding and skillful efficiency.

Preliminary superconscious states experienced without revelations of Self-knowledge may be temporary, and the devotee's attention may return to involvements with conditioned states of awareness. When established in Self-understanding and empowered with confidence, one can live wisely, practice meditation successfully, and progressively awaken through the stages of spiritual growth. While knowledgeable, focused personal endeavor can produce favorable results, enlightenment is more quickly realized when the devotee contemplates the reality of God and aspires to know and realize it.

If we do not have a clear concept of God when we begin our enlightenment quest, if we sincerely endeavor to live righteously and engage in spiritual growth practices, as intellectual capacities improve and superconscious realizations unfold, the presence and reality of God will definitely be experienced.

Poor physical health or illness; laziness; doubt; negligence; procrastination; philosophical confusion; failure to experience progress; attachments to pleasure or to behaviors, circumstances, or relationships which provide it; misperceptions; and various kinds of mental distractions, are obstacles to effective living and success in meditation practice. When these conditions are influential, they may contribute to thoughts and feelings of grief, anxiety, inability to relax, and irregular breathing patterns, making it difficult if not impossible to concentrate. If we ardently aspire to Self-knowledge, mental distractions and their effects can be eliminated by devoted meditation practice and contemplation on God. Mental distractions can also be minimized and mental and emotional calm restored by cultivating thoughts and feelings of friendship, compassion, and happiness, and by imagining and contemplating ideal possibilities.

When meditating, mental distractions can be avoided by practicing specific procedures and techniques that require complete attention and involvement. These may be devotional prayer, breath awareness, listening to a mantra, concentration on the vital centers in the spinal pathway followed by concentration at the spiritual eye center between the eyebrows, using procedures for circulating life force through the vital centers, or any procedure or technique that is known to be helpful to quieting the mind. These procedures and techniques are explained in a later chapter.

Superconscious states also impress the mind, leaving entirely constructive traces or memories, just as thoughts, emotions, and sensory perceptions leave their influential mental impressions. Mental impressions that result from superconscious perceptions and from apprehension of the "four categories of higher knowledge" inhibit ordinary mental impressions acquired by mundane experiences and produce permanent, beneficial mental and personality changes. With complete awakening to Self-knowledge, even the memories of superconscious influences are eventually dissolved.

Because superconscious perceptions and influences

favorably impress the mind, regular meditation practice to the stage of mental peace and clear awareness is recommended. If exceptional perceptions are absent during meditation, consciously resting for twenty minutes to an hour or more in the clear state of awareness elicited by meditation practice is extremely beneficial. It provides deep rest for the organs of the body, unstresses and enlivens the nervous system, and provides vivid experience of pure awareness devoid of mental and emotional influences. Regular, repeated exposure of the mind and physiology to the constructive influences of superconscious states results in psychological transformation, improved health and functional abilities, and progressive spiritual growth. As the mind is purified and the nervous system is refined, awakened vital forces circulate more easily and soul awareness flows more freely.

The impulse of the soul to have awareness expanded is increasingly influential when mental and physical conditions which restrict it are minimized and removed. Some truth seekers, hoping to experience a sudden shift of awareness that will result in enlightenment, unwisely ignore helpful advice regarding lifestyle guidelines, psychological transformation, and meditation practice. While it is true that these actions will not cause enlightenment, they can prepare the body and mind to be receptive to it. A purified mind and a refined nervous system allow easier awakening to enlightenment.

With awakening of soul capacities, enhanced functional abilities may also unfold. These may include the ability to exercise extrasensory perceptions, expand awareness to omnipresence, have desires or intentions immediately fulfilled, and to accomplish any chosen purpose. These abilities are not supernatural powers or gifts bestowed by a benevolent deity as a reward for good behavior or diligent endeavor; they are natural soul capacities to be used wisely. Because they are only indications of soul awakening, fascination with them should be avoided if spiritual progress is to be uninterrupted. They should primarily be used to purify the mind and successfully accomplish complete God-realization.

Knowledge of the mundane realm and our relationship to it enables us to live effectively. Knowledge of our true nature and of inner causes that produce outer effects makes possible unrestricted living.

Seek realization of God, and live righteously; and all of your personal needs will be unfailing supplied.
— *The Gospel According to Saint Matthew 6:33*
Modern translation

Eight

Lifestyle Routines and Spiritual Practices for Complete Well-Being and Rapid, Authentic Soul Unfoldment

To be healthy, happy, and in the flow of good fortune we need to be spiritually awake and in harmonious accord with the rhythms of life. Passive, confused, or mere wishful thinking will not produce the results we desire. We need to know our relationship with the Infinite and so live our lives that we are responsive to its impulses and it is responsive to us. Health, happiness, affluence, and soul unfoldment is facilitated when we choose constructive lifestyle routines that enable us to have the full support of nature's life-enhancing actions and influences, including practices that illumine the mind and allow our innate qualities to spontaneously unfold.

To accomplish worthwhile purposes, it is necessary to have a clearly defined vision of possibilities for their accomplishment. It is then easier to choose and maintain thoughts, moods, and choices of relationships and actions which make possible effective living and physical, mental, emotional, and spiritual fulfillment, and satisfying personal circumstances. Writing our clearly defined purposes in a personal notebook or journal confirms our decision to accomplish them. It also attunes our awareness and mental processes to Cosmic Mind, with which, in the

FOR YOUR PERSONAL JOURNAL

Write Your Clearly Defined Purposes and Commitments to Constructive Actions

1. Specify how much of your time, attention, energy and personal resources you have allocated to:

a. Work ______________________________
b. Leisure ____________________________
c. Family _____________________________
d. Social relationships and activities ___________
e. Self-improvement studies and practices ________
f. Charitable endeavors or service _____________
g. Philosophical reflection ________________
h. Prayer and meditation _________________
i. How much money is required for your personal needs, the well-being of others for whom you are responsible, and your worthwhile projects and activities? ____________________
j. What percentage of your income or resources do you regularly give to religious, cultural, or other causes that you consider to be worthwhile? _____

2. What do you need to do to improve your attitudes, behaviors and personal circumstances? Begin to do what is necessary.

3. Engage in possibility thinking, using your powers of creative visualization to see ideal outcomes.

4. Write an affirmation to clearly define your resolve to live effectively and grow spiritually.

relative realms, we are always in relationship. Our determined intention empowers us to think and act effectively and our attunement with Cosmic Mind attracts supportive response. We thus help ourselves by our choices of actions and Cosmic Mind, in which the universe resides, provides us with circumstances, events, relationships, and resources which support our constructive endeavors and make possible fortunate outcomes.

Decide how much of your time, attention, energy, and personal resources to allocate for work, leisure, family and social relationships and activities, self-improvement studies and practices, charitable endeavors, philosophical reflection, prayer, and meditation. Decide how much money is required for your personal needs, the well-being of others for whom you are responsible, and your worthwhile projects and activities. Give a portion of your financial resources to individuals in need or to well-managed group endeavors that are efficiently organized with a clear mission-purpose and which effectively meet the physical, psychological, moral, and spiritual needs of others. Write your decisions in your notebook and adhere to them.

Think Only of Your Highest Good and Envision Desired Outcomes

When writing your clearly defined purposes, think in terms of your highest good and the highest good of others who may be influenced by your actions. Think about how your actions will affect society and the environment. Renounce all thoughts, moods, personal behaviors, relationships, and actions which are not consistent with your soul aspirations and goals, while adopting modes of

FOR YOUR PERSONAL JOURNAL

Write Your Commitment to a Daily Self-Care and Focused Meditation Practice Routine

1. How many hours do you sleep? ________________

2. What is your early morning self-care routine?

   ____

3. What is your regular exercise routine?

   ____

4. What is your wholesome dietary regimen? ________

   ____

5. When do you meditate? ________________
   a. Your procedure and routine ________________

   ____

   b. Average duration of practice ________________

6. If you meditate twenty minutes to reduce stress and for physical and psychological benefits, once a week, meditate for 30 minutes or one hour.

7. What is your choice of regular reading or study material for acquiring useful knowledge and to improve your understanding of your relationship to God? ________________________________

8. Always remember that you are an immortal, spiritual being and live from that understanding. Acknowledge the innate, divine nature of others.

behavior which will have entirely constructive effects. Be attuned to the elevating and illuminating qualities of nature by your choices of thinking and behavior. Neutralize restlessness by cultivating inner peace. Avoid laziness and inertia.

Use your powers of creative imagination. Envision and feel yourself to be physically and psychologically healthy, happy, creatively functional, successful, prosperous, and spiritually enlightened. Your soul capacities will be awakened and self-defeating habits and psychological tendencies will be weakened and banished. You will learn to express wisely, freely, and enjoyably without fear and devoid of awareness-diminishing attachments.

The ability to imagine possibilities is a soul capacity to be used creatively and constructively. When used in relationship to the mind, body, and mundane circumstances, it enables us to cause effects and to attract desired circumstances. When used to expand awareness, it enables us to assume viewpoints unrestricted by conditioned mental states and allows the experience of higher realities. The key to constructive use of imagination is willingness to be responsible for personal actions that will cause corresponding effects.

Some people are so fixated in their egocentric viewpoints and beliefs of limitation that they are reluctant to imagine alternative possibilities. Because of habit or fear of making decisions, they choose restricted circumstances instead of the complete freedom that could be theirs by imagination, Self-acceptance, and right endeavor.

Think about the possibilities available to you. If you were enlightened, how would you think? How would you feel? What would be your physical condition? What behaviors would be normal for you? What foods would you choose to eat? What would be your personal circumstances? What kind of personal relationships would you have? What would you be doing that would be different from what you are now doing? With new insights, live like an enlightened person. Instead of passively hoping for future improvement or indulging in fantasies and wasting time and resources in useless endeavors and relationships, organize your thinking and your priorities. Decide what is most important for your highest good and proceed with courage and enthusiasm.

Daily Self-Care and Spiritual Practice Routines

Even when we have good intentions, habit and conditioned modes of thinking and behavior, and other matters which require our attention, may cause us to neglect our daily self-care and spiritual practice routines.

Self-care routines can include a balanced schedule of activity, rest, and exercise, and choosing a natural, wholesome diet, preferably vegetarian.

We function more effectively when work, recreation, and social activities conform to a planned schedule. Regular hours of sleep rest the mind, regenerate the body, and ensure high energy levels.

The exercise routine might include hatha yoga or t'ai chi, performed in the morning before meditation, or later in the day to counteract stress and enliven body and mind with vital forces that are awakened and circulated by these practices. Brisk walking, exercise with moderate weights, or any other activity that increases respiration and blood circulation and improves muscle tone and strength, should be scheduled at least three or four times a week.

A balanced, nutrition-rich, low calorie vegetarian diet is most suitable for overall health and spiritual awareness, and is especially recommended to support a program of self-transformation that includes intensive meditation practice. If you are not yet knowledgeable about these beneficial practices, it will be worthwhile to read informative literature. It will also be helpful to read about Ayurveda (life-knowledge), the several thousand year-old wellness system used to balance the basic mind-body constitution by various natural means: attitude adjustment, behavioral modification, meditation, food choices, and cleansing and rejuvenation procedures.

Meditation should be practiced daily, preferably in the morning while the mind is still calm after sleep and before thinking about secular activities. If desired, another meditation session can be included in the late afternoon or early evening to elicit physical relaxation and unstress the nervous system.

In your personal notebook or journal, also write affirmations that clearly define your resolve to live effectively and awaken spiritually. Write them with soul-felt conviction and calmly and forthrightly speak them aloud until vivid awareness of the truth of your words saturates your consciousness, mind, and body. The following affirmation is but an example:

> I acknowledge that I am a flawless expression of God's consciousness and that total knowledge of God and of cosmic processes is within me. With firm resolve and unwavering faith I live with conscious intention to assist myself to complete well-being and spiritual growth.

Outline your self-care and meditation routines, modifying or supplementing them as desired or needed. Write what you will do to conform your life to what is ideal for you. Keep a record of your progress.

Remember that because the universe is a continuum, a seamless manifestation of the energies of God's consciousness, your mental states, states of consciousness, and actions influence everything in it. The more spiritually conscious you are, the more constructive are your influences. As you awaken through the stages of spiritual growth, all souls are benefited and planetary consciousness is refined by your enlightenment. In accord with your inner guidance, talents, and resources, assist others who are responsive to your help to live more consciously and effectively and provide them with information for their spiritual education. While meeting the needs of others at a level which is most appropriate, be conscious of serving their inner, divine nature. Be compassionate but not sympathetic. Care about people without assuming their pain or problems. Endeavor to assist people in need to be as knowledgeable, strong, and competent as possible. Pray for their good fortune and the fulfillment of their spiritual destiny.

Meditate for Physical and Psychological Health and Progressive Spiritual Growth

Even if you do not presently aspire to complete spiritual enlightenment, meditate daily for physical and psychological health and the gradual, progressive spiritual growth that will naturally occur. Schedule fifteen to twenty minutes once or twice a day to meditate to the stage of physical relaxation and mental calm, and rest in superconscious tranquility for several minutes. Superconsciousness is superior to ordinary states of consciousness and beneficially impacts the mind and physiology. Your thoughts will be more orderly; emotions will be calmed; stress will be reduced; the body's immune system will be strengthened; biologic aging processes will be slowed; regenerative energies will be awakened and will circulate freely; and the body's organs, glands, and systems will function more efficiently. You will be more alert, think more clearly, have more energy, and be enabled to live more effectively.

For this twenty minute meditation session, choose a word or word-phrase as your mantra to be used every time you meditate. "God"..."Om"..."peace"..."joy"... or any word that is attractive to you is suitable. A word-phrase might be "Om-God"..."I am–pure consciousness"..."I rest–in wholeness"... or one that you choose for yourself.

The chosen word or word-phrase is not to be used as an affirmation. Its purpose is to attract and focus attention so that thoughts are excluded from awareness and concentration flows effortlessly.

Decide when and where you will practice and do it at the same time every day. Sit upright on a comfortable chair, with spine and neck erect. You may sit in a cross-legged posture on the floor or any comfortable place if you prefer (you may want to sit on a pillow or a folded blanket for comfort). The meditation posture should be pleasant and easy to maintain so that attention is not distracted. With closed eyes, look slightly upward, at and through the place between your eyebrows, and be aware inside your head. Avoid strain when you do this.

- Pause for a few moments to be centered, poised, and relaxed. Imagine yourself as abiding in a boundless ocean of conscious life. Let your sense of independent selfhood dissolve and be receptive to apprehending wholeness. Silently acknowledge your relationship with God. Be aware of your normal breathing rhythm.
- When inhalation occurs, mentally listen to your chosen word. When exhalation occurs, mentally listen to it. If using a word-phrase, mentally listen to the first part of the phrase with inhalation and the second part of the phrase with exhalation. You need not mentally recite the word or word-phrase. Let it arise in your awareness synchronized with your body's normal breathing rhythm.
- Continue listening to your chosen word or word-phrase until it ceases to manifest and you are established in a thoughtless, tranquil, aware state.
- Rest in this state of tranquil, clear awareness for the duration of the practice session.
- When inclined to conclude the session, open your eyes and be still for a few moments. During this transition phase, maintain your meditative calm. Mentally and spiritually renewed, resume your normal activities.

By meditating this way, attention is removed from involvement with physical and mental processes and the soul's innate urge to have awareness restored to wholeness can be influential in facilitating the unfoldment of its qualities and enlargement of its capacities. This is why spiritual growth spontaneously occurs as a result of regular meditation practice.

Meditate as a self-care regimen even when you may feel inclined to neglect it. Meditators who include religious or devotional practices in their routines are more inclined to maintain a regular schedule.

When meditating, remain aware of your purpose and of the progressive stages of practice. Your purpose is to have your awareness restored to wholeness by removing attention from distracting influences. The progressive stages of practice are (1) stability of the meditation posture; (2) physical relaxation and mental calm along with balanced flows of the body's vital forces; (3) internalized attention; (4) concentration on the word or word-phrase; (5) unwavering concentration or pure meditation; (6) the peak experience—tranquil awareness devoid of thoughts or emotional influences.

Immediately after meditation practice, while your mind is calm, is an ideal time to write in your notebook or journal. You may also want to devote a few minutes to pray for others, discern solutions to problems, or envision possibilities for more effective living or accomplishment of major purposes. Or you may choose to immediately resume your normal activities.

Avoid anxiety about results of meditation practice. Meditate regularly and let the benefits naturally unfold in the course of time. If thoughts and emotional states distract your attention, quiet them by more focused concentration and practice of meditation techniques. As you become proficient you will notice that, as breathing becomes slower and refined, thought processes and emotions are calmed. Restless, irregular breathing disturbs flows of vital force in the body and causes mental fluctuations and mood changes. When breathing is naturally slow and refined, mental actions and emotions are restrained and calmed. You will learn by experience how and why the meditation process works. While an intellectual grasp of the process is helpful, only regular experience in the silence will result in meaningful insights.

When planning to practice for fifteen to twenty minutes, allow extra time to prolong the session on occasions when you are settled in a soul-satisfying superconscious state and the meditation process is flowing smoothly.

Every day, meditate more deeply
than you did the day before.
— *Paramahansa Yogananda*

Nine

In the Sanctuary of the Soul: Meditation Techniques and Advanced Practices That Unveil Knowledge and Liberate Consciousness

To quickly unfold superconscious states, meditate long and deep with special techniques and advanced practices. Instead of meditating for fifteen to twenty minutes for physical and psychological health and gradual spiritual growth only, schedule longer and more frequent practice sessions. If you are a beginning meditator, maintain your short daily sessions and include a thirty minute session once a week until you acquire more proficiency in practice. If you have been meditating on a regular schedule for several months, extend your daily session to thirty minutes or an hour, adding another daily session after another few months.

Be sure to balance meditative practices with intentional living routines and maintain a keen interest in accomplishing purposes and performing duties. In this way you will avoid becoming so preoccupied with investigating subjective states of consciousness that you lose interest in secular life. When meditating, concentrate completely on knowing the truth about yourself and awakening to God-realization. When not meditating, remain established in Self-knowledge and live skillfully and effectively. It is not necessary to completely withdraw from the world and from activities and relationships to be spiritually free. When we clearly comprehend that we are spiritual beings in a consciousness-energy-manifested universe sustained and ordered by a Higher Intelligence, we can maintain inner realization and live successfully in relationship to the world and its processes.

The advanced meditation techniques and practices described in this chapter have been taught by many enlightened teachers through the ages. Become proficient in all of them and include them in your practice sessions as recommended.

Having a private meditation sanctuary can be helpful. This may be a small, secluded room, or place set aside in a larger room. Consecrate it for the purpose of meditation and philosophical reflection. Install a comfortable chair. If desired, have a picture of your guru or of saints whose spiritual attainment inspires you. Keep your sacred space simple and clean. When you go there, thoughts of secular matters will be replaced by thoughts of your relationship with God. Aspiration to Self-knowledge will be nurtured and superconscious meditation will more easily be experienced.

If you sincerely want to be fully awake to your true nature and know the reality of God, meditate with focused intention impelled by devotion to God and firm commitment to accomplish your purpose. Remain alert and observant. Practice techniques to elicit physical relaxation and mental calm, then direct your attention to discovery of what you want to know about God, your relationship to God, and cosmic processes. Contemplate clear states of consciousness and awaken to them. Directing attention in this way is meditative contemplation, which is successfully accomplished when concentration and meditation culminates in insight or realized experience as determined by your aspiration and focused intention. Examples of accomplished meditative contemplation are (1) discernment of knowledge; (2) actualization of the soul qualities of peace, happiness, compassion, wholeness, and exceptional functional skills; (3) vivid experience of refined superconscious states and transcendent realizations.

When the intellectual faculty is unveiled and purified, superior powers of discernment can be demonstrated. When intuition is unveiled, the truth about whatever is examined can be directly and immediately known. When awareness of our true nature is no longer obscured by illusions and delusions, we are enlightened; our Self-revealed knowledge is reflected in our illumined mind and expressed through our refined physical body. When permanently established in this realization and consciousness is no longer influenced by the qualities of nature or of cosmic forces, we are liberated.

A More Intentional Meditation Routine and Supplemental Techniques to Practice

Bathe or wash your hands and face and take a few sips of cool water. Wear loose, comfortable clothing. Go to your meditation place with anticipation. Assume an alert, upright meditation posture.

- Pause for a moment or two to get settled and comfortable. With stomach muscles relaxed, take two or three deeper than normal breaths, then exhale. Relax your face, neck, and shoulder muscles. Be poised and peaceful.

- Look into the spiritual eye between your eyebrows.
- Acknowledge the innate divinity of all souls.
- Acknowledge the truth of your being, knowing and sensing that you are a flawless expression of Supreme Consciousness and that all knowledge of God and of the processes of the cosmos is within you.
- Think of God as God is real to you. Intuitively sense that you are residing in a field of boundless, omnipresent, pure consciousness.
- If you have a guru, think of your guru with reverence. Be thankful for that relationship.
- Let any remaining sense of independent selfhood dissolve. Acknowledge that God's wholeness includes you. Feel your awareness to be absorbed in oneness.
- Pray for the ability to meditate effectively and to experience soul unfoldment.
- Listen to your mantra, or direct your attention to your chosen point of focus as you are inclined or inspired to do. If you have been initiated into the practice of another meditation technique, use it. During longer meditation practice sessions, use the techniques described in this chapter. Continue until your attention is internalized and meditation flows easily.
- Rest in the alert, tranquil state for as long as it persists. Let your innate intelligence direct the meditation process. While still established in the tranquil state, contemplate for the purpose of having insights or to experience more refined levels of superconsciousness. At the innermost level of your being you are pure and whole. Be aware of and experience your purity and wholeness. If thoughts and memories intrude, banish them by a gentle

act of will or resume practice of a technique until your awareness is again clear and tranquil.

- Conclude your practice session when you feel inclined to do so. Remain seated with eyes closed for a few moments. Intuitively sense that you are in perfect harmony with the rhythms of life. Have faith that as you are thus in harmony with universal processes, you are included in their actions. Be established in soul-aware conviction that events, circumstances, and relationships will spontaneously and appropriately unfold to nurture you and support your worthwhile endeavors and actions.
- Acknowledge all souls everywhere and wish for them their highest good. Know that just as the currents of God's grace contribute to your total well-being and fulfillment, so they contribute to the total well-being and fulfillment of everyone. Be happy at the core of your being. Be thankful. Affirm with confidence:

> Established in Self-revealed knowledge, I am whole in God. Wisdom-directed, I live freely, easily, and enjoyably in a God-governed, supportive universe. The understanding and happiness I now have, I lovingly wish for others.

When meditating for thirty minutes to an hour, practice your preliminary routine until calm, and rest in the silence. When your attention begins to waver or the mind becomes restless, practice your preferred technique or one of the following techniques to renew your interest and deepen your practice. For three weeks, besides your usual technique, practice a different supplemental technique each week to become familiar with it.

Moving Life Force Through the Chakras

When your breathing is natural and slow and the mantra is synchronized with inhalation and exhalation, look more intently into the spiritual eye and be aware inside your spine and brain.When you breathe in, listen to your mantra and feel a subtle current of life force moving smoothly from the base of the spine upward through the chakras and into the brain. When you breathe out, listen to your mantra and feel the subtle current gently flowing downward. Feel the life force flowing like liquid light, pulled up when you breathe in and flowing downward of its own accord when you breathe out.

The key to effective practice of this technique is to relax into it and acquire proficiency by experience. While you may also visualize the flow of current in the early stages, it will be more effective to learn to feel the current moving as you inhale and exhale. Mild, pleasurable sensations may be experienced in the spine and brain as the current moves. If extremely pleasurable sensations occur, enjoy them without being overly involved with them. If spontaneous surges of current move in the spinal pathway, remain relaxed and still. Let the vital forces flow without allowing sensations of any kind to disturb your physical poise, mental calm, or meditative concentration.

As you practice this technique, you may notice that you are breathing more slowly and a little deeper than usual. Continue to feel the flows of life force until your attention is internalized, then give your attention only to your mantra until it fades and meditation proceeds naturally. Breathing will then be slow, refined, and barely noticeable. There may be occasions of automatic pause after exhalation, during which thoughts are absent and tranquil awareness prevails. By learning to remain poised in the tranquil stillness, it will persist when the normal breathing rhythm is resumed. Do not attempt to restrain the breathing pattern. Observe the natural adjustments of states of consciousness that correspond to physiological changes as deep relaxation and mental calm is experienced. Calmly observe whatever occurs.

As you become proficient in practicing this technique you will notice that, as your breathing becomes internalized, air is not moving forcefully through your nose and lungs but seems to be moving through the spinal pathway. Breathing will occur naturally and attention will be entirely inward. This procedure awakens dormant energies in the lower chakras, magnetizes the spine and brain, harmonizes the movements of vital forces in the body, and takes attention toward the higher brain centers. When flows of vital force in the body are balanced, mental processes become serene and refined, instinctual drives and subconscious tendencies become dormant, and superconscious states are more easily experienced.

Flowing Awareness Through the Chakras

Sit upright and look into the spiritual eye. Be aware in the spinal pathway and brain. Feel the aliveness in the spine and interior of your skull. Locate the vital centers. Starting at the base chakra, feel the chakra and mentally chant Om once. Move up to the second chakra, feel it and mentally chant Om once. Continue upward through the third, fourth, and fifth chakras, feeling the sensation at each center while chanting Om. Be aware at the spiritual eye and mentally chant Om. Be aware in the higher brain and mentally chant Om. Pause for a moment, then descend through the chakras, feeling the sensation and mentally chanting Om at each one. Pause for a moment. Repeat the process six to ten times. When inclined to conclude practice of the technique, ascend through the chakras once more, look intently into the spiritual eye, and let meditation flow naturally.

Meditating on Inner Sound and Light

Place the palms of your hands over your eyes. With your thumbs, gently close the ear openings by pressing the tragus (the small cartilage in front of the opening of the ears) to exclude outside sounds.

Look intently into the spiritual eye and listen for sounds in your ears. Listen in the right ear, then the left ear, then in both ears. When beginning, you may not hear any sounds. Eventually you will hear subtle, electrical noises. Start with the sound you first hear, gently endeavoring to hear finer sounds behind it. Continue until the inner sound flows steadily. Consider this sound to be an aspect of the Om vibration that pervades the universe. Merge your awareness in the sound until you are one with it, floating in the ocean of cosmic consciousness.

With your awareness merged in inner sound, gaze into the spiritual eye, looking at and through it into the distance of inner space. Steady gazing improves concentration and calms the mind. If you see light in the spiritual eye, observe it. Peer at it steadily with alert attention. Do not let your attention wander. If mental chanting of Om during the early stages of practice helps to keep your attention focused, do this. Eventually, cease mental chanting and listen to the inner sound.

You may see a golden orb centered with a dark blue light. In the blue light you may see a brilliant white light. Gold is the color of the light of Om. Blue is the color of the light of the all-pervading consciousness of God. The white brilliance is the source of all aspects of light.

Initial light perceptions may vary—perhaps only a gold or blue light, or a ball of bright light like a full moon against a dark background. Or you may see a tunnel of light that seems to extend far into the distance. If you do, you may wish to experiment by gently surrendering yourself to it, moving through the tunnel to perceive and experience whatever is to be revealed to you. If visions of places and people occur, know these to be mental phenomena and disregard them. Rest in the light and the Om vibration for a while, then aspire to experience pure consciousness, transcending both light and sound.

After sitting for a while, if the muscles of your arms and shoulders become tired, remove your hands from your eyes and ears and rest them in your lap, continuing your inner exploration of light and sound.

If you are sitting for an extended duration of time, you may also wish to explore the sounds of the life force frequencies emanating from the chakras. To do this, feel the base chakra and listen to detect the subtle sound that emanates from it. Move up to the second chakra and listen to its sound frequency. Continue through the chakras to the higher brain, then settle into contemplation of the sound of Om while looking into the spiritual eye.

Expanding Awareness to Omnipresence

It is usually recommended that meditation be practiced to remove awareness from mental processes. This technique, however, utilizes self-guided visualization to the stage where intentional visualization ceases and spontaneous meditation occurs.

Flow your attention up through the chakras and look into the spiritual eye. Visualize a dark blue ball of light. Identify your awareness with it. Imagine that you are the ball of conscious, blue light. As conscious, blue light, expand until you fill the skull, then the body, then expand beyond the outlines of the body so that it is contained within you. Expand until you fill the room where your body sits, then until the room is within you. Expand until the building in which your body sits is contained within you. Continue to expand, including people, creatures, nature, communities, cities, towns, and finally Planet Earth in your field of awareness. Visualize the planet drifting in the endless space of your enlarged awareness. As conscious blue light, continue to expand until the Milky Way Galaxy, with its billions of flaming suns, 100,000 light years from edge to edge, is within your field of awareness. Still expanding, include the billions of galaxies in the universe in your field of awareness. Intuitively acknowledge the astral and causal realms interpenetrating the physical universe. Acknowledge that physical, astral, and causal realms exist in Universal Mind. Contemplate the field of primordial nature: Om, cosmic particles, space, and time. Contemplate the origin of Om, God as the Oversoul. Contemplate the Field of Pure Consciousness. Continue meditative contemplation until you feel inclined to conclude the practice session.

Experiment with these processes until you discover what works best for you. Avoid being a slave to mechanical practice of meditation. Procedures are to be used for your spiritual benefit, to enable you to adjust states of consciousness at will and to experience superconscious states and have transcendent perceptions.

When you have acquired proficiency in the practice of these meditation techniques, use them as you feel inclined during longer meditation sessions. When meditating for an hour or more, start with your usual preliminary routine and rest in the silence when you experience the tranquil state. When attention wavers, use another technique until calmly concentrated, and rest in the silence. Continue like this until you decide to conclude your practice.

Refined Superconscious States and Liberation of Consciousness

Remember to remain alert and attentive when meditating. Avoid daydreaming, preoccupation with ideas and meditative perceptions, and passive, nearly unconscious states. If, after meditation, you have no memory of the experience, you were not as alert as you should have been.

If you have a devotional nature, let your devotion burn like a bright flame to support your aspiration while improving your powers of discriminative intelligence. If you are by nature more intellectual, purify your intellect, cultivate devotion to God, and be steadfast in your resolve to awaken to complete enlightenment.

When meditating, when you are so absorbed in light,

FOR YOUR PERSONAL JOURNAL

Write Your Meditation Schedule and Practice Routines

Time of day__________ Duration of practice __________

Regular routine ____________________________________

____

____

Schedule for practicing supplemental techniques:

First week ____________________________________

Second week ____________________________________

Third week ____________________________________

Fourth week ____________________________________

Schedule for practicing longer meditation sessions:

( ) Each week ( ) Every two weeks ( ) Once a month

Duration of practice ____________________________________

Extended practice routine ____________________________________

____

____

____

____

____

sound, or any other object of contemplation that your awareness is completely merged in it, you are experiencing *samadhi* (oneness) with the support of that with which your awareness is identified. Although this is a spiritually beneficial preliminary state, it should eventually be transcended. The ideal is to experience oneness without the support of an object of concentration. The preliminary state of oneness purifies the mind and refines the body, but if it becomes the preferred experience, the meditator may neglect to awaken to advanced states. Enjoyment of meditative experiences that results in attachment to them is an obstacle to progress.

Other perceptions and experiences to which one might become attached include visions of various kinds, the pleasure caused by flows of life force in the spinal pathway and elsewhere in the body, and ecstatic states experienced when energy flows become intense or when Self-revealed knowledge of higher realities unfolds. While meditative experiences that enhance spiritual awareness are of value, it is best not to cling to any perceptions or experiences that are transitory. Many devotees interfere with their spiritual progress and delay enlightenment because they erroneously believe that they have accomplished their ultimate aim, or choose to remain attached to conditions which, while enjoyable, are not redemptive.

Because preliminary superconscious states are modified by thoughts and emotions, you may sometimes wonder whether or not you are actually experiencing superconsciousness. With gentle persistence, you will experience clear awareness with only subtle thoughts and emotions present. When clear, tranquil awareness prevails, thoughts and emotions are no longer perceived and meditative contemplation can be practiced without effort.

Refined superconscious states purify and illumine the mind and result in Self-knowledge and God-realization. When superconsciousness prevails after meditation practice, cosmic conscious states progressively unfold until complete realization of the truth of God and life processes is permanent. Soul awareness is liberated.

A seeker of truth who was intent on enlightenment went to a highly respected teacher to have his attainment verified.

The teacher inquired, "Please tell me what you have realized."

The seeker said, "When I am meditating, I am peaceful and my thoughts are subtle. The experience is very enjoyable."

"That's good," the teacher replied, "but you haven't yet got it. Please continue your practice."

After six months, the seeker reported: "When my meditations are deep and long, I am very happy. Sometimes, in my ecstasy, it seems that I am one with everything and I am almost overwhelmed with thoughts and feelings of unconditional love for everyone."

"That's good," the teacher responded, "but you haven't yet got it. Please continue your practice."

A few weeks later, the seeker said, "When I am meditating, I have no thoughts. There are no perceptions of 'otherness' of any kind. My experience is that of exceptional clarity and wholeness that I cannot put into words. After meditation, clarity and wholeness remain undiminished."

"That's *very* good!" the teacher acknowledged. "Now you have it! I have a favor to ask of you. Will you please, let me be your student? Teach me to awaken to that blessed state."

Chapter Ten

The Final Revelation

Absolute liberation is the goal of the spiritual aspirant whose commitment to the enlightenment path is total. Individuals with weak or inconstant resolve tend to compromise: to be satisfied with limited salvation which affords them a degree of temporary comfort.

The terms *liberation* and *salvation* have the same meaning. To be liberated is to have consciousness removed from mental restrictions that formerly obscured it and its knowledge. The word origin of salvation (Latin *salus*, whole, healthy) implies the ideal of having the ordinary human condition healed of error, death, ignorance of the truth about life, and various kinds of impurity. This meaning is also implied in the German words *Heil*—healing—and *heilig*—the holy or sacred, the source of transformative influences that reclaims wholeness. In many enlightenment traditions the ordinary human condition is viewed as a sickness that can be cured by awakening and actualizing soul qualities, acquiring useful knowledge, attitude adjustment, behavior modification, moral living, psychological transformation, and faith in a higher power.

Limited salvation is a condition of being sufficiently healthy-minded and spiritually aware to temporarily be free from discomfort, grievances, and misfortune. For people who tend to be attached their self-conscious nature and ordinary social relationships, a condition of limited freedom is, to them, often acceptable. However, when deep-seated unconscious drives, compelling desires, or psychological conflicts become influential, physical weakness or illness may again be experienced. Circumstantial challenges may seem to be overwhelming and apathy and despair may prevail. When aspiration to further spiritual awakening wanes and attention becomes overly involved with ordinary secular interests, one may tend to fall back into former states of consciousness and the modes of behavior which correspond to them.

Limited salvation is a confined condition because (1) Self-knowledge is not yet complete; (2) awareness is still somewhat restricted by erroneous notions, illusions, subconscious conditionings, and personality-based views of oneself in relationship to God and nature.

A common mistake made by many who are somewhat spiritually awake, is to erroneously believe their condition of limited salvation to be final freedom when, in fact, they have not yet overcome or transcended their limitations. Although they may enjoy degrees of cosmic consciousness, experience ecstasies and have clairvoyant perceptions, be able to demonstrate exceptional abilities, have some mastery of their mental states, states of consciousness, and circumstances, and may be able to perform what others might consider to be miracles, their spiritual attainment is only partial. They have attained a "semi-divine condition" which indicates a level of spiritual growth to eventually be surpassed.

A dedicated devotee on the enlightenment path will not err in thinking the way—the awakening process and the practices which facilitate it—to be the goal itself. Nor will such a one be enamored of novel theories or glamorous involvements which distract attention from the important matter of focused commitment to self-transformation and transcendence of mundane conditions which blind the soul to Self-knowledge. Neither preoccupation with philosophical opinions, superficial investigation of various methods and practices, constant seeking out of new teachers, excessive interaction with other devotees however sincere, nor reliance on the help of saints long gone from this world, can be of any real value to one who ardently aspires to be enlightened—to be fully awake.

Absolute liberation is accomplished when delusions, illusions, and psychological characteristics which inhibit the free flow of consciousness are absent and Self-revealed knowledge of the reality of God is fully and permanently unfolded. The reliable way to awaken to absolute liberation is to be steadfast in resolve to accomplish it as quickly as possible while living a wholesome, purposeful life and engaging in spiritual practices that will allow the soul's innate impulse to have awareness restored to wholeness to be freely expressive.

Every truth seeker who is willing to surrender the limitations of the self-conscious condition—the illusional sense of independent selfhood—in favor of unbounded God-realization can awaken to it by right personal endeavor and God's influential, redemptive grace.

Glossary

An understanding of the meanings of the following words and subjects will be helpful to more fully comprehend the ideas and themes presented in this book. Definitions of Sanskrit words are included for readers who are familiar with yoga and its practices.

Absolute Transcendent, Supreme Consciousness.

actualize To make real or to bring into manifestation. Abilities are actualized when they are expressed or demonstrated. Goals are actualized when they are accomplished. Purposes are actualized when they are fulfilled.

advaita Nonduality. The teaching that everything in manifestation is an expression of Supreme Consciousness.

agnosticism A theory that does not deny the existence of God but denies the possibility that God can be known and maintains the opinion that only perceived phenomena are objects of exact knowledge. See *atheism* and *deism*.

ashram A quiet, secluded abode for study and spiritual practice. An ashram provides a supportive environment in which spiritual aspirants can live close to nature without distractions. Only elevating influences should prevail, to nurture soul qualities and encourage their unfoldment.

astral realm The realm of life forces and electricities. Souls come into physical incarnation from the astral realm and return to it between earth sojourns. Spiritually advanced souls may pass through it to continue their awakening in a finer causal realm or transcend it to be removed from involvement with all aspects of primordial nature. See *causal realm*.

atheism Disbelief in or denial of the existence of God. See *agnosticism* and *deism*.

Atman Also *Atma*. The true, permanent essence of every person and creature. The divine Self realized by an accomplished seeker on the spiritual path. *Paramatman* (*para*, beyond; *atman*, the individualized Self)) is unmodified Supreme Consciousness.

avatar The emergence of divine power and qualities in human form. A full incarnation of God for the purpose of infusing planetary consciousness with divine influences. Avatars are believed to occasionally play dramatic roles, or their spiritual state may be unrecognized by those with whom they associate. Their redemptive work is in accord with the innate inclinations of divine impulses expressing as evolutionary trends and actions. The "universal avatar" concept is that the reality of God abides equally in and as every soul and that divine capacities are actualized as individual and collective human consciousness becomes illumined.

avidya Not-knowledge, in contrast to *vidya*, knowledge of God's reality and its aspects and categories of manifestation.

Ayurveda *Ayur*, life; *veda*, knowledge. India's several thousand year-old system of wellness. According to folklore, this knowledge was taught to man by the gods. Chinese Medicine is also said to have been taught to man by the gods, and there is a similarity of procedures. Both include an examination of the patient's pulse, temperature, skin condition, eyes, psychological characteristics, behavior, and other factors for diagnostic purposes. Ayurveda uses diet, herbs, water therapy, massage, attitude training, behavior modification, detoxification regimens, and meditation along with other specific procedures to restore the body to a condition of balance. Ayurvedic therapies are prescribed to balance the three subtle element-influences (space-air, *vata;* fire-water, *pitta*; and water-earth, *kapha*) which govern physiological functions and influence psychological states. The *Charaka Samhita*, an Ayurvedic text, lists over five hundred herbs and describes their medicinal uses. Knowledge of Ayurveda passed from India to Mediterranean countries, and finally to the West. During the years of British rule, state patronage resulted in the decline of Ayurvedic practice in the urban centers of India, although it continued to be the treatment of choice among rural populations. Currently, there are several Ayurvedic colleges in India and some in other countries, and scientific research is underway to investigate and validate many of these wellness procedures.

Babaji *Baba*, father; *ji*, a suffix used at the end of a name to indicate respect. In Asia, many saints who are venerated are referred to as Baba or Babaji. Mahavatar (*maha*, great; *avatar*) is the name used to refer to an enlightened saint who revived the ancient kriya yoga teachings and practices and introduced them into public consciousness in India during the nineteenth century. A woman saint may be addressed as Mataji (*mata*, mother; *ji*, who is reverenced).

Bhagavad Gita Holy or Divine Song. From *bhaj*, to revere or love; *gita*, song. A scripture treasured by millions of people in which the author portrays Krishna as a divine incarnation who teaches to his disciple Arjuna "the eternal way of righteousness" and the yogas of knowledge, selfless service, devotion, and meditation. Frequent reading of the Bhagavad Gita can purify the mind and awaken innate spiritual qualities.

Bhagavan Lord, that which rules. Also, one who is endowed with the spiritual attributes of infinite spiritual power, righteousness, glory, splendor, knowledge, and renunciation.

bhakti Fervent, devoted love for God which can result in God-realization and clear perception of the innate divinity of every person and creature. Love purifies the mind and awakens soul capacities and qualities.

bliss The unadulterated soul joy of awareness of pure being, rather than mental happiness or an emotional mood.

Brahma The expanding, projecting aspect of the Godhead which results in full manifestation of nature. *Vishnu* is the name given to the aspect of God which preserves and maintains the universe. *Shiva* is the name given to God's transformative aspect which dissolves forms and circumstances to allow new expressions. Shiva is also considered to be Supreme Consciousness. *Shakti*, the creative energy of Supreme Consciousness, is thought of as it's feminine expression, the creative energy that manifests and enlivens the worlds.

brahmacharya *Brahma*; divine; *charya*, going. Disciplined regulation of vital forces, mental and emotional tendencies, and behaviors to conserve and transmute energies, freeing them and the devotee's attention for intentional living and dedicated spiritual practices. A *brahmachari* is a person dedicated to disciplined living; also one whose attention is God-centered whether cloistered or living a secular life.

Brahman The Supreme Reality, the Absolute.

Buddha A seer who lived in northern India about 500 B.C. Of royal birth, as a young man he became troubled when he learned of the sufferings of the average person in society. After marrying, and fathering a son, he left home to seek higher knowledge. Following a duration of ascetic yogic practice he adopted "the middle way" of reasoned moderation and awakened to illumination of consciousness. The word *buddha*, is used to refer to one who is enlightened. After his illumination he walked through the Ganges Valley for almost half a century, preaching and forming a society of renunciates. He taught love, nonhatred, dedication to truth, the elimination of wishful thinking, and nondependence upon externals. Buddhism teaches that illumination is the realization of the True Self which is common to all, rather than a state of consciousness to be attained.

buddhi From the verb-root *budh*, to know. The faculty of discernment, the intellectual capacity. When, by discernment, the totality of consciousness is apprehended, one is a buddha, an enlightened being. Because all souls are expressions of Supreme Consciousness, all have a buddha nature. When the soul awakens to full realization of its true nature, it is spiritually free.

capacity The capability to receive or contain. The power or ability to use skills and accomplish purposes. Right living and spiritual practices increase one's capacity to apprehend and experience the reality of God and to accomplish purposes.

causal realm The realm or field of magnetism and electric properties preceding astral and physical manifestation. Souls reside here before returning to astral incarnation or while awakening to transcendent levels. See *astral realm.*

chakra An astral vital center through which *pranas* (life forces) flow. The first chakra, at the base of the spine, represents the earth element. Influenced by apana prana, its taste is sweet, its color is yellow, and its sound is like the noise of frantic bees. The psychological state related to the first chakra is characterized by restlessness and insecurity. Its name *muladhara* means "foundation."

The second chakra, at the sacral region of the spine, represents the water element. Influenced by apana prana, its taste is astringent, its color is white, and its sound is that of a flute. The psychological state related to the second chakra is characterized by desire and sensuousness. Its name *svadhisthan* means "abode of the self" because kundalini (the spiritually unawakened soul's dormant potential energy) is confined here.

The third chakra, at the lumbar region of the spine, represents the fire element. Influenced by samana prana, its taste is bitter, its color is red, and its sound is that of a harp. The psychological state related to the third chakra is characterized by self-centered inclinations and strong powers of will. Its name *manipura* means "the city of gems."

The fourth chakra, at the dorsal region of the spine, represents the air element. Influenced by the primary prana, its taste is sour, its color is blue, and its sound is that of the peal of a gong. The psychological state related to this chakra is characterized by aspiration to spiritual growth which may be frustrated because powers of discernment are sometimes flawed. Its name *anahata* means "unstruck sound."

The fifth chakra, at the cervical region of the spine opposite the throat, represents the ether element. Influenced by udana prana, its taste is pungent, its color is grey or misty with sparkling points of light, and its sound is that of thunder or the ocean's roar. The psychological state related to the second chakra is characterized by inspiration to acquire knowledge. Its name *vishudda* means "pure."

The sixth chakra is the spiritual eye between the eyebrows which reflects the light from the medulla oblongata at the base of the brain. Its name *ajna* means "command."

The seventh chakra is in the higher brain. Its radiance is brilliant white. Its name *sahasrara* means "thousand rayed."

In the Bhagavad Gita story, the five Pandava brothers represent the positive qualities of the element essences (*tattwas*) of the five lower chakras as indicated by their names. *Sahadeva* (devotion, always shining, day) represents the earth element essence of the first chakra. *Nakul* (stillness of the mind, night) represents the water element essence of the second chakra. *Arjuna* (purity of mind and heart, the aspiring devotee, fiery will and self-control for personal purposes) represents the fire element influence of the third chakra. *Bhima* (dauntlessness, control of vital forces—*pranayama*—control of the forces of nature, endless strength, formidable) represents the air element essence at the fourth chakra. *Yudhisthira* (righteousness, dharma, steadfast and firm) represents the ether element essence of the fifth chakra. See *prana* and *Bhagavad Gita.*

chitti Individualized consciousness. When transformations characteristic of ordinary awareness are quieted, illumination of consciousness is experienced.

Christ From Latin *christus*, derived from Greek *kristos* (*khristos*, anointed, and *kriein*, to anoint). For secular use the word was used to refer to the religious rite of anointing with oil. In some philosophical systems, the aspect of God pervading the universe is referred to as Christ Consciousness. Thus, one who has realized the all-pervading reality of God may be said to be Christ Conscious.

consciousness Ordinarily considered the state of being conscious or aware. The metaphysical meaning is the reality of God's being and the reality of our individual being.

cosmic consciousness Awareness of life as wholeness which may be partial or complete. It may unfold gradually or suddenly, accompanied by knowledge which is Self-revealed. Cosmic consciousness can be nurtured by renouncing egocentric attitudes and self-conscious behaviors, aspiration to spiritual growth, prayer, superconscious meditation, and reliance upon God. When meditative superconscious states continue during ordinary waking states, cosmic consciousness is nurtured. Cosmic conscious states can also suddenly emerge without preliminary indications of its unfoldment.

Cosmic Mind Cosmic Mind-Substance or Universal Mind. The omnipresent mental field of which all individualized minds are an aspect or part. Mind, whether Cosmic or individualized, includes a field of awareness, self-sense (egoism), the intellect or discerning aspect, and the aspect which processes information. Through its individualized mind, each embodied soul is in relationship to Cosmic Mind. Mental states, with thoughts, desires, intentions, and karmic conditions, interact with Cosmic Mind which is responsive and tends to manifest corresponding conditions and circumstances.

deism Belief that God created the universe but is removed from it, has no influence on phenomena, and provides no supernatural revelation. See *agnosticism* and *atheism.*

delusion An erroneous or invalid belief or opinion due to intellectual error or imperfect or incomplete discernment. The initial error of the intellect is to mistaken the Self to be mind or matter. All other delusions and their consequences result from this. See *ego* and *illusion.*

deva A shining one, a god. Gods, (*devas*) and goddesses, (*devis*) are considered to be spiritually radiant souls dwelling in subtle or celestial realms. The gods may also be considered to be cosmic forces that regulate universal processes and can be invited to influence human affairs.

dharma That which upholds, maintains, and supports creation and contributes to evolution. To live in harmony with evolutionary processes is to live in accord with dharma: righteously, appropriately, correctly. To live in accord with the order of the universe and to adhere to one's destined path is to fulfill one's personal dharma.

disciple Word origin: Latin *discipulas*, pupil, from *discere*, to learn. A disciple is committed to learning, as an adherent of a philosophical system or spiritual tradition. See *guru.*

ego Erroneous presumption of independent existence because of the veiling or clouding of awareness that causes an illusional sense of being separate from God. Inaccurate Self-sense is the basis of egoism. The soul then erroneously presumes itself to be separated from its origins, identifies with objective realms, and is unable to comprehend subjective realms and transcendent realities. See *delusion* and *illusion.*

ether Space comprised of fine cosmic forces which are not yet matter but have the potential to manifest as matter; the first of five material element manifestations comprising the field of manifested nature. The four other subtle element influences are air, fire, water, and earth which express as their corresponding material manifestations. The five subtle element influences are the true essences (*tattwas*) of the manifest universe. Physical manifestation of the elements occur when half of one subtle element influence is mixed with one eighth part of the other four subtle element influences.

God The Supreme Being; the outward manifestation of Divine Consciousness expressing in the direction of universal manifestation. The Oversoul, the Cosmic Soul.

guna A quality, attribute, or characteristic of consciousness expressing as a cosmic influence that regulates nature's forces. The three gunas are the constituent aspects of the whole of nature that determine its actions. *Sattva guna* contributes to purity and luminosity. *Rajas guna* contributes to movement and transformation. *Tamas guna* contributes to heaviness and inertia and its influence clouds the mind.

guru Teacher. That which removes darkness or ignorance of the truth. The light and reality of God is the true guru that removes darkness or ignorance from the mind and consciousness of the disciple. An enlightened teacher is a *Satguru (sat*; the truth of being; *guru*, revealer). See *disciple.*

heaven Originally a cosmological term that identified a region of the universe but which also came to function as a vehicle of religious idealism. In ancient Near Eastern thought, heaven identified a region of the observable cosmos which pointed beyond itself to a realm or field of transcendence. In ancient Greek mythology, Zeus dwells on Mount Olympus. The Old Testament refers to heaven as God's abode from which sovereign rule is exercised and to which the faithful righteous are finally welcomed. The New Testament reflects a modified version: heaven is God's creation in which God resides as well as a condition of blessedness experienced by the spiritually prepared. Various sects have their own concepts of heaven and its opposite place or condition. Illusion-free understanding allows one to directly experience the truth that one's degree of Self-knowledge and God-realization determines personal circumstantial conditions.

illusion Misperception; failure or incapacity to accurately apprehend what is subjectively or objectively observed. One may then presume to know when one does not. Illusions believed to be true are delusions; both distort awareness and contribute to mental and emotional conflict. When illusions are renounced or removed, soul awareness is restored to wholeness. See *ego* and *delusion.*

imagination The ability to mentally image or visualize what is not present to the senses. Creative imagination differs from daydreaming or fantasy only in degree. Disciplined imagining enables one to clearly define mental concepts and imagine the possibility of desired near and future circumstances.

Ishwara Or *Isvara*. The aspect of God which governs and regulates creation. Referred to as the lord or ruling influence.

japa Repetition of any of the names of God or a mantra for the purpose of cultivating devotion and improving meditative concentration. A *japmala* is a string of beads used to count the repetitions or to more completely involve the meditator's attention during prayerful contemplation. The rosary used by devout Catholics serves this purpose.

jivanmukta One who is soul *(jiva)* liberated (*mukta*) while embodied. Although traces of karma may remain, the soul is free because Self-realized. Future actions of the liberated soul are then determined by it's innate intelligence and responsiveness to God's guiding grace rather than by karmic compulsion. A *paramukta* (*para*, beyond; *mukta*, free) is supremely liberated: without delusions, illusions, or karmic compulsions and not subject to influences of cosmic forces. See *salvation.*

jnana Knowledge, especially knowledge of God.

jyotish The study and application of knowledge of astronomy and astrology. In an ancient text, the *Kaushitaki Brahmana*, it is indicated that in 3100 BCE Vedic scholars had knowledge of astronomy for determining favorable times for religious and other ceremonies. Vedic astrology calculates planetary positions in relationship to fixed signs. Certain gemstones are believed to radiate forces similar to those of the major planets, hence the reason for recommending the use of gemstones to counteract or to strengthen planetary influences. In this system the recommended gemstones are ruby for the sun's influence; pearl or moonstone for the Moon influence; red coral for the influence of Mars; emerald for the influence of Mercury; yellow sapphire for the influence of Jupiter; diamond for the influence of Venus; blue sapphire for the influence of Saturn; and onyx and cat's eye for the influences of the nodes of the Moon. It is recommended that gems to be used for therapeutic or other helpful purposes be prescribed by an enlightened astrologer. The recommended weights are usually two or more carats. They should be obtained under favorable astrological circumstances, set in a ring or pendant at a chosen time, purified by the use of herbs and other substances, offered to one's chosen aspect of God, appropriate mantras should be chanted, and the item of jewelry put on at the appropriate time of a prescribed day. Gems should also be set in a prescribed metal, such as gold or silver, as metals are also considered to impart their special influences.

kalpa A cycle or duration of time. See *yuga.*

karma From the verb-root *kri*, to act; to do; to make [happen], the principle of causation. The thoughts one habitually thinks, mental states, states of consciousness, and actions determine personal experiences. Karma also refers to the accumulation of influential mental and emotional conditionings in the mind and physical body.

kaya-kalpa *Kaya*, strong physical body; *kalpa*, cycle or duration of time. An Ayurvedic regimen prescribed for physical

with the meditator's intention, contemplation can result in (1) awareness of oneness with the object contemplated; (2) direct realization of pure consciousness.

metaphysics From Greek *meta*, beyond or after; *physika*, the physical side of nature (Aristotle's treatise so titled). The word is now commonly used to refer to philosophical theories about matters beyond the realm of relative phenomena.

moksha Also *mukti*. Liberation of soul consciousness. Liberation is accomplished when awareness is devoid of delusions and illusions. See *jivanmukta* and *salvation.*

mudra A symbolic gesture. Also, a yogic procedure used to regulate and enliven the body's life forces and to control or master involuntary processes.

nadi A channel or pathway through which prana flows in the body at the astral level. *Ida* is the left channel along the spinal pathway; the lunar influence. *Pingala* is the right channel; the solar influence. The central channel is *sushumna*, the pathway through which the meditator's vital forces are directed when practicing certain kriya yoga meditation techniques or similar procedures.

nadi shuddhi Purification of the nadis by pranayama practice or when prana flows spontaneously after kundalini is awakened. See *nadi, prana,* and *pranayama.*

Nirguna-Brahma Supreme Consciousness without attributes or qualities. *Saguna-Brahma* is Supreme Consciousness expressing with attributes and qualities.

ojas The most refined form of energy as matter that strengthens and vitalizes body and mind and enhances awareness. It is considered to be the final product of food transformation. It is also increased by stress management, conservation and transmutation of physical and mental energies, mental calm, a wholesome lifestyle, spiritual practices, and superconscious states. See *Ayurveda* and *brahmacharya.*

Om (*Aum*) The creative force-sound-current emanating from the Godhead from which all manifestations of nature are produced. Om is the pure meditation mantra to contemplate and from which all other mantras derive their potencies.

omnipotence Unlimited power.

omnipresence Present everywhere.

omniscience All knowing.

parabda karma Residual karmic impressions which can cause effects. If their potential effects are known to be harmless, they can be allowed to express, thus weakening and eliminating their motive force. They can be neutralized and dissolved by constructive living, surrendered prayer, meditation, repeated superconscious episodes, and the superior force of God-realization. See *karma.*

paramahansa *Param*, beyond or transcendental; *hansa*, swan. One considered to be a spiritual master: a free soul no longer bound by rules because actions are always wisdom-impelled and spontaneously appropriate. As the swan has an earthly abode but can soar free in the sky, so a paramahansa dwells in the world but is not influenced by or confined to it. According to mythology, the swan is able to extract milk from water. A paramahansa is able to partake of the divine essence while living without restrictions in the world.

Paramahansa Yogananda Disciple of Sri Yukteswar and the guru of Roy Eugene Davis. Born in India, January 5, 1893, he lived in the United States from 1920 until his passing on March 7, 1952. His most famous book is *Autobiography of a Yogi.*

prakriti The field of nature consisting of subtle element influences and their manifestations and discernible characteristics. *Purusha* is the divine force enlivening nature.

prana *Pra*, forth; *an*, to breathe. Life force pervading nature. It expresses as various frequencies to perform specific life support functions. When pranas flow harmoniously, health prevails; when their flows are imbalanced, discomfort or ill health is possible. Pranayamas regulate the force and circulation of prana in the body, usually by regulated breathing, and allows its expansion. The physical body is nourished and the mind is energized by the soul's life force. The five aspects of prana in the body are (1) upward flowing *udana prana*, seated in the throat it contributes to speech; (2) *prana*, seated in the chest it regulates breathing; (3) *samana prana*, seated in the stomach and intestines it regulates digestion, assimilation, and biochemical processes. (4) *apana prana*, seated below the navel it regulates elimination of the body's waste products; (5) *apana prana* pervades the body and regulates the movements of other aspects of prana. See *chakras*.

pranayama *Pran[a]*, life force; *ayama*, not restrained, freely flowing. Pranayama can occur naturally when the mind is calm and one is soul-centered or it can be facilitated by regulated pranayama practice.

prayer Petitioning prayer is the act of asking God for help or for benefits of some kind, the results of which are demonstrated as desired circumstances or satisfying states of consciousness. Prayer can be mental or verbal. Surrendered prayer results in a turning away from self-sense to allow apprehension and unfoldment of soul qualities and direct perception of transcendent realities. People of all faiths have experienced the transformational effects of surrendered prayer. Some have realized God directly by prayer without knowledge or practice of any other technique or procedure.

rasayana *Rasa*, taste, juice, elixir, or essence; *ayana,* pathway, to circulate, or to have a home, place, or abode. In Ayurveda, rasayana treatment is a means of restoring the immune system so that body fluids circulate to find their natural places. Herbal compounds prescribed for rasayana therapy are many and varied. One preparation is of raw sugar, clarified butter, Indian gall nut, Indian gooseberry, dried catkins, Indian pennywort, honey, nutgrass, white sandalwood, embrella, aloewood, licorice, cardamom, cinnamon, and turmeric. The ashes of certain metals and gemstones may also be used. See *Ayurveda* and *kaya-kalpa.*

reincarnation The doctrine of return, of being born into another body after a duration of rest in the astral realm. The belief that the soul can be attracted to the physical realms because of mental or emotional attachments or because its states of consciousness are compatible with them. Reincarnation can also be from causal to astral realms. See *astral* and *causal realms.*

renunciation Relinquishment of mental and emotional attachments to things, circumstances, emotional states, actions, and the results of actions while selflessly involved in relationships, activities, and spiritual practices.

salvation The condition of being liberated from the effects of causes of pain or discomfort because of Self-knowledge and the overcoming, removal, or transcendence of karmic conditions, delusions, and illusions by personal endeavor and God's grace.

samadhi From the verb-root *sam*, to put together. When mental modifications no longer fragment or disrupt the flow of soul awareness, it is restored to wholeness and samadhi is experienced. Samadhi is not an unconscious or trance state, it is a state of clear, unfragmented awareness.

samkalpa Determination, will, or intention to cause a thing, event, or circumstance to manifest.

samkhya To enumerate. *Samkhya philosophy* defines and describes the categories, stages, and orderly processes of cosmic manifestation from the Field of Pure Consciousness to the material realms.

samsara *Sam*, together; verb-root *sri*, to flow). The continuing transformations of nature. Unenlightened people involved in its shifting currents are influenced by its actions. Enlightened souls remain established in Self-knowledge and flow with circumstances and observe their actions.

samskara Mental impression, imprint, a memory. Perceptions, whether of objective circumstances or of subjective incidents such as thoughts, feelings, or insights result in impressions or memories. If influential, they can disturb mental and emotional peace by causing fluctuations and transformations in one's mind and awareness. They can have potential for pain or pleasure or be neutral or constructive. Mental impressions made by superconscious influences are entirely constructive. Spiritual practices resist, weaken, and dissolve samskaras. See *karma.*

samyama Perfected or accomplished contemplation, when concentration, meditation, and identification with the object of contemplation is simultaneous.

Sanatana Dharma The eternal way of righteousness. The impulses innate to consciousness which incline the actions of nature to be harmonious and fulfilling and which contribute to soul awakening and unfoldment. As knowledge of the eternal way of righteousness is revealed or discovered, our lives have the full support of nature and spiritual growth is spontaneous.

Sanskrit The refined, perfected, or polished language from which approximately one hundred Indo-European languages, including English, are derived. Prominent in India during the Vedic era and used today by some scholars and students of philosophy. The Sanskrit alphabet is considered to be a mantra: a sound-phrase of spiritual significance and power which reveals the seed-frequencies of creation. Every word or sound (*shabda*) has a power (*shakti*) which conveys the sense which is inseparably related to the sound. Sanskrit word-sounds have an innate power to convey their inner meaning. The sound-element behind the audible sound is the fundamental sound (*sphota*). Audible or written Sanskrit can accurately reveal the meaning of what is read or heard, and contemplation of the subtle sound-element or seed-power reveals its true essence. Sanskrit mantras are believed to be unique for the purpose of facilitating spiritual awakening. Mantras derive their potency from Om, the primordial sound current emanating from the Godhead and expressive throughout the universe. See *Om* and *mantra*.

sat Being, reality, truth. The Absolute is referred to as *Sat-Chit-Ananda*: Reality-Consciousness-Bliss.

Self The true essence of being. See *Atman*.

Self-realization Conscious knowledge-experience of one's true nature. The Self of every person and creature is pure consciousness. When identified with mental processes and the body and its sensations and sense objects, the Self becomes outwardly involved and partially forgets its real nature. Self-remembrance, ordered living, and spiritual practice elicits (brings forth) soul awakening and Self-realization: the restoration of awareness to its original, pure state.

shakti Cosmic creative force enlivening nature. Also, the aspect of kundalini which, when aroused, vitalizes the body and contributes to psychological transformation, physical vitalization, and progressive spiritual awakening and growth.

shaktipat The transmission of creative force from one person to another, usually from the guru to a disciple; also its spontaneous awakening because of sustained aspiration to enlightenment, devotion, spiritual practices, and grace.

siddha A spiritually perfected or accomplished person.

siddhi Innate spiritual power or ability which can unfold and be instrumental to the accomplishment of purposes of all kinds, especially to awakening to Self-realization.

soul An individualized ray of God's consciousness reflected from the field of primordial nature that mistakenly presumes itself to be independent of God. The soul's illusional state of consciousness has to be purified and transcended to have its awareness restored to wholeness. See *salvation* and *jivanmukta*.

spiritual eye In the forehead, between and above the eyebrows; the reflected light from the medulla oblongata at the base of the brain. Through the spiritual eye the meditator directs attention and moves awareness into subtle realms.

Sri Yukteswar Disciple of Lahiri Mahasaya and the guru of Paramahansa Yogaṇanda. (May 10, 1855 to March 9, 1936.)

swami A member of the ancient monastic order reorganized by the philosopher-seer Adi (the first) Shankara in the eighth century. A swami has renounced all mundane attachments, selflessly works for the highest good of others, and [usually] engages in spiritual practices to awaken to God-realization.

tantra From *tan*, to extend or expand. *Tantric philosophy* explains the processes of creation and dissolution of the universe, procedures for relating to universal forces and accomplishing the aims of life, how to awaken and express innate abilities, and meditation techniques to clear the mind and facilitate awakening to ultimate Truth-realization.

tapasya From the verb-root *tap*, to burn. Spiritual endeavor by means of concentrated, disciplined austerity with ardent devotion to the ideal of Self-realization. Intentional living that includes dedicated spiritual practice effectively removes all physical and mental obstacles to spiritual growth.

tattva The true essence of a thing. The true essence of a thing can be known by *samyama*, meditative contemplation.

Transcendental Field Pure, Absolute Consciousness.

turiya The fourth state of consciousness transcending the three commonly experienced states of deep sleep, the dream state, and ordinary waking states. Superconsciousness.

Upanishads *Upa*, near; *ni*, down; *sad*, to sit. A collection of texts considered sacred with origins in oral traditions. Centuries ago, in India, the disciple would live with the guru in a retreat environment and sit near to learn. Among the several texts, the ones for which Shankàra wrote commentaries are referred to as the Greater Upanishads because of their general appeal. The Lesser Upanishads contain yogic instruction meant for devotees prepared to study them; one such treatise is the *Shandilya Upanishad* written by an ancestor of Lahiri Mahasaya.

vasana Latent tendency. When inclined in the direction of actualization, vasanas cause fluctuations in individualized awareness. Latent tendencies are neutralized by constructive living and spiritual practices. See *vritti*.

Veda Revealed knowledge. The Vedas contain the revelations of the ancient seers; the Upanishads offer philosophical explanations of the Vedas.

Vedanta The summing up of the wisdom of the Vedas. The final revelation is that Supreme Consciousness is the cause, reality, and support of all that is.

vritti Process, action, fluctuation, wave, or modification occurring in the mental field when *vasanas* (impulses arising from tendencies to action) stir them into motion. Vrittis are calmed by dispassionate observation of circumstances when engaged in ordinary activities and relationships, meditation practice, and superconsciousness. See *vasana.*

Vyasa An ancient sage believed to have arranged many of the Vedic works in their present form. Vyasa is probably a name used by several sages over a period of centuries.

yama-niyama *Yama*, restraint. By resisting and regulating destructive impulses, their opposite characteristics are cultivated and perfected: harmlessness; truthfulness; honesty; constructive use of vital forces and soul capacities; and insightful renunciation which makes possible appropriate relationships and use of natural resources. *Niyamas*, not-restraints, include inner and outer cleanliness or purity; soul contentment in all circumstances; disciplines to facilitate psychological transformation (see *tapasaya*); study and meditation for Self-knowledge and contemplation of higher realities; and surrender of self-consciousness (the illusional sense of independent selfhood) in favor of awakening to awareness and realization of transcendent realities.

yoga (1) to yoke, to bring together one's awareness with unbounded Consciousness (soul awareness with God) by using specific practices that remove restrictions from mind and awareness; (2) any of the various systems used for this purpose; (3) samadhi, the culmination of yoga practice, the meaning used in Patanjali's *yoga-sutras*. Preliminary samadhi states are clear states of soul awareness identified with the object of contemplation. Pure samadhi is the free state without the support of objects of awareness.

The practice of yoga may vary to meet the needs of the practitioner's psychological temperament and personal capacities. *Hatha* (from the verb-root *hath*, to oppress or restrain) *yoga* practitioners endeavor to control physiological and psychological states by the application of postures (*asanas*), pranayamas, and meditative practices. *Bhakti yoga* is the devotional approach to apprehending the all-pervading reality of God. *Karma yoga* is the way of mental renunciation of the results of actions rather than the avoidance of the performance of necessary actions. *Jnana* (gyana) *yoga* is the way of intentional use of powers of discriminative intelligence to discern the truth of Self and of God and nature. *Raja* (royal, kingly) *yoga* is the eightfold way of perfecting (1) the five external disciplines; (2) the five internal disciplines; (3) meditation posture; (4) mastery of the body's life forces and mental processes; (5) internalization of attention; (6) concentration; (7) meditation; (8) superconscious states and samadhi. The terms kriya yoga, laya yoga, kundalini yoga, and others that are sometimes used, indicate specialized practices which may be emphasized and are included in the basic yogic systems.

yoga sutras *Sutra*, from the verb-root *siv*, to sew. Sutras are oral or written teachings in concise form, a thread of ideas or statements that convey the message. The *yoga sutras* written by the sage Patanjali (circa 200–500 CE) comprise an exposition of yogic philosophical principles and practices that were known and used for many centuries prior to his writing about them. Patanjali's *yoga sutras* are presented in four parts: (1) definitions and descriptions of samadhi states and how they are to be accomplished; (2) kriya yoga, the practices; (3) an explanation of supernormal powers (siddhis), their constructive applications, and emphasis on their use for the purpose of removing restrictions to Self-realization; (4) the final stages of meditative contemplation and liberation of consciousness.

yuga An Age or designated duration of time. Centuries ago, Vedic astronomer-seers taught a theory of electric time-cycles to explain the effects of cosmic forces on human beings and evolutionary trends that affect Planet Earth. The ascending cycle which is one-half of a complete 24,000 year cycle is described as (1) a 1,200 year Dark Age during which most human beings are intellectually deficient and spiritually unaware; (2) a 2,400 year Age of Awakening during which intellectual powers and spiritual awareness increase and electric and magnetic properties of nature are discovered anew; (3) a 3,600 year Age when intellectual powers are keen and knowledge of nature's forces is common; (4) a 4,800 year Age when many on the planet can comprehend the reality of God: an era of planetary enlightenment. We are currently in the early stages of an ascending 2,400 year Age which emerged in 1700 CE and will continue until the year 4,100 when the 3,600 year ascending Mental Age will begin. The duration of the Ages, in ascending order, are actually 1,000, 2,000, 3,000, and 4,000 solar years. Transition phases between them, during which influences of the preceding Age are superseded by the superior influences of the emerging Age, are ten percent of the preceding Age.

The theory of electric time-cycles is based on the presumed influences of the energies from the center of our galaxy on our solar system and on the mental and intellectual faculties of its human inhabitants. When our Sun and its planets are nearest to the galactic center, human powers of perception are refined, intellectual abilities are pronounced, soul knowledge is more easily unveiled, and enlightenment is the common condition. When we are more distant from the galactic center, human powers of perception are weak, intellectual powers are minimal, soul awareness is obscured, and ignorance of the facts of life prevail. Regardless of the Age in which one lives, when aspiration to Self-discovery is impelling, spiritual growth and illumination of consciousness are possible.

Because of a mistake that occurred many centuries ago in calculating the progressions of the Ages, many people still believe that we are currently in a Dark Age cycle that will continue for several hundred thousand years. Observation of the present state of collective human consciousness and awareness of scientific discoveries and technological advances made within the past few hundred years, indicate that we are indeed in an Age of rapid intellectual and spiritual awakening.

NEW AGE PUBLICATIONS

ART AND SCIENCE OF PSYCHIC HEALING—*Larry M. McDaniel* and *Phyllis G. McDaniel*
ISBN: 81-7822-030-x Code 030x

ART AS A GUIDE TO SELF-REALIZATION—*J. Donald Walters*
ISBN: 81-7822-028-8 Code 0288

AYURVEDIC COOKING—*Ramesh Patel*
ISBN: 81-7822-016-4 Code 0164

THE AYURVEDIC DIET (The Ancient Way to Health Rejuvenation and Weight Control)—*Dr. Dennis Thompson*
ISBN: 81-7822-014-8 Code 0148

THE BOOK OF BUDDHAS (Ritual Symbolism used on Buddhist Statuary and Ritual Objects)—*Eva Rudy Jansen*
ISBN: 81-7822-055-5 Code 0555

THE BOOK OF CHAKRA HEALING—*Liz Simpson*
ISBN: 81-7822-043-1 Code 0431

THE BOOK OF HINDU IMAGERY (Gods and their Symbols)—*Eva Rudy Jansen*
ISBN: 81-7822-056-3 Code 0563

BREATHE FREE (Nutritional and Herbal Care for Your Respiratory System)—*Daniel Gagnon* and *Amadea Morningstar*
ISBN: 81-7822-018-0 Code 0180

CHAKRA ENERGY MASSAGE (Spiritual Evolution into the Subconscious through Activation of the Energy Points of the Feet)—*Marianne Uhl*
ISBN: 81-7822-004-0 Code 0040

ENERGETIC HEALING (Embracing the Life Force)—*Arnie Lade*
ISBN: 81-7822-005-9 Code 0059

THE EXPANDING LIGHT COOKBOOK (Vegetarian Favorites)—*Blanche Agassy McCord*
ISBN: 81-7822-052-0 Code 0520

FENG SHUI FOR THE BODY (Balancing Body and Mind for a Healthier Life)—*Daniel Santos*
ISBN: 81-7822-012-1 Code 0121

THE GREATNESS OF SATURN (A Therapeutic Myth)—*Dr. Robert E. Svoboda*
ISBN: 81-7822-057-1 Code 0571

THE HEALING HANDBOOK (A Spiritual Guide to Healing Yourself and Others)—*Tara Ward*
ISBN: 81-7822-034-2 Code 0342

HEALING THE FUTURE (The Journey Within)—*Deepak Kashyap*
ISBN: 81-7822-039-3 Code 0393

THE HEART OF HEALING (Body, Mind and Spirit)—*Caroline Latham*
ISBN: 81-7822-019-9 Code 0199

THE HINDU MIND (Fundamentals of Hindu Religion and Philosophy for All Ages)—*Bansi Pandit*
ISBN: 81-7822-007-5 Code 0075

HOMEOPATHY (A Comparative Materia Medica)—*Santosh Kumar*
ISBN: 81-7822-040-7 Code 0407

HOMEOPATHY (For Common Ailments)—*Robin Hayfield*
ISBN: 81-7822-044-x Code 044x

HOW TO ACHIEVE INCREDIBLE RESULTS BY INSPIRATION —*P. Vatsala* and *T. Gokulan*
ISBN: 81-7822-035-0 Code 0350

HOW TO MASTER CHANGE IN YOUR LIFE (Sixty-Seven Ways to Handle Life's Toughest Moments)—*Mary Carroll Moore*
ISBN: 81-7822-036-9 Code 0369

HYPNOSIS FOR CHANGE—*Josie Hadley* and *Carol Staudacher*
ISBN: 81-7822-029-6 Code 0296

THE INTUITIVE WAY (A Guide to Living from Inner Wisdom)—*Penney Peirce*
ISBN: 81-7822-008-3 Code 0083

KAILASH MANSAROVAR (Diary of a Pilgrim)—*Nilesh D. Nathwani*
ISBN: 81-7822-054-7 Code 0547

LIFETIME WEIGHT CONTROL (Seven Steps to Achieving and Maintaining a Healthy Weight)—*Patrick Fanning*
ISBN: 81-7822-022-9 Code 0229

LIVING MEANINGFULLY, DYING JOYFULLY—(The Profound Practice of Transference of Consciousness)—*Geshe Kelsang Gyatso*
ISBN: 81-7822-058-x Code 058x

LUMINOUS ESSENCE (Exploring the Body Consciousness)—*Daniel Santos*
ISBN: 81-7822-033-4 Code 0334

MAGNETIC HEALING (Advanced Techniques for the Application of Magnetic Forces)—*Buryl Payne*
ISBN: 81-7822-002-4 Code 0024

THE MYTHS OF DEATH, REBIRTH AND RESURRECTION (The Wisdom of the Serpent)—*Joseph L. Henderson* and *Maud Oakes*
ISBN: 81-7822-031-8 Code 0318

NATURAL HEALTHCARE AT HOME (Doctor Mum's Quick Reference Guide)—*Kathy Duerr*
ISBN: 81-7822-017-2 Code 0172

A NEW LOOK AT PAST LIVES—*Judy Hall*
ISBN: 81-7822-015-6 Code 0156

THE ORIGINAL REIKI HANDBOOK OF DR. MIKAO USUI—*Frank Arjava Petter*
ISBN: 81-7822-020-1 Code 0201

PENDULUM HEALING HANDBOOK (Complete Guidebook on How to Use the Pendulum to Choose Appropriate Remedies for Healing Body, Mind and Spirit)—*Walter Lubeck*
ISBN: 81-7822-003-2 Code 0032

PRESCRIPTION FOR STRESS—*Kenneth Matheny* and *Christopher J. McCarthy*
ISBN: 81-7822-032-6 Code 0326

PSYCHIC POWERS: A PRACTICAL GUIDE (Awaken Your Sixth Sense) —*Melita Denning* and *Osborne Phillips*
ISBN: 81-7822-051-2 Code 0512

QUANTUM-TOUCH (The Power to Heal)—*Richard Gordon*
ISBN: 81-7822-009-1 Code 0091

THE SELF-REVEALED KNOWLEDGE THAT LIBERATES THE SPIRIT —*Roy Eugene Davis*
ISBN: 81-7822-050-4 Code 0504

SELF-TRANSFORMATION THROUGH MUSIC—*Joanne Crandall*
ISBN: 81-7822-024-5 Code 0245

THE SPIRITUAL BASIS OF REAL PROSPERITY—*Roy Eugene Davis*
ISBN: 81-7822-053-9 Code 0539

SPIRITUAL HEALING (Doctors Examine Therapeutic Touch and Other Holistic Treatments)—*Dora Kunz*
ISBN: 81-7822-011-3 Code 0113

STEP-BY-STEP HEAD MASSAGE—*Eilean Bentley*
ISBN: 81-7822-045-8 Code 0458

STEP-BY-STEP YOGA FOR STRESS RELIEF—*Swami Shivapremananda*
ISBN: 81-7822-046-6 Code 0466

STHAPATYA VED-VASTU SASTRA—*Niketan Anand Gaur*
ISBN: 81-7822-042-3 Code 0423

STRESS-FREE WORK WITH YOGA AND AYURVEDA—*Vinod Verma*
ISBN: 81-7822-000-8 Code 0008

SUPERCONSCIOUSNESS (How to Benefit from Emerging Spiritual Trends)—*J. Donald Walters*
ISBN: 81-7822-026-1 Code 0261

TANTRA WITHOUT TEARS—*Christopher S. Hyatt* and *S. Jason Black*
ISBN: 81-7822-027-x Code 027x

TAPPING YOUR INNER STRENGTH (How to Find the Resilience to Deal with Anything)—*Edith Henderson Grotberg*
ISBN: 81-7822-010-5 Code 0105

THEORIES OF THE CHAKRAS (Bridge to Higher Consciousness) —*Dr. Hiroshi Motoyama*
ISBN: 81-7822-023-7 Code 0237

THIRTY-FIVE GOLDEN KEYS TO WHO YOU ARE AND WHY YOU'RE HERE—*Linda C. Anderson*
ISBN: 81-7822-037-7 Code 0377

TIBETAN POWER YOGA (The Essence of All Yogas a Tibetan Exercise for Physical Vitality)—*Jutta Mattausch*
ISBN: 81-7822-006-7 Code 0067

UNCONDITIONAL BLISS (Finding Happiness in the Face of Hardship) —*Howard Raphael Cushnir*
ISBN: 81-7822-013-x Code 013x

UNDERSTANDING YOUR BODY ALIGNMENT (Health and Longevity) —*Harmon Hathaway*
ISBN: 81-7822-001-6 Code 0016

VASTU VIDYA (The Indian Art of Placement)—*Juliet Pegrum*
ISBN: 81-7822-047-4 Code 0474

VEDIC HEALTH CARE SYSTEM (Clinical Practice of Sushrutokta Marm Chikitsa and Siravedhan Highlighting Acupuncture)—*Binod Kumar Joshi, Geeta Joshi* and *Ram Lal Sah*
ISBN: 81-7822-041-5 Code 0415

WORKING ANGER (Preventing and Resolving Conflict on the Job) —*Ronald T. Potter-Efron*
ISBN: 81-7822-025-3 Code 0253

THE YOGA COOKBOOK (Vegetarian Food For Body and Mind) —*Sivananda Yoga Vedanta Centres*
ISBN: 81-7822-048-2 Code 0482

THE YOGI (Portraits of Swami Vishnu-devananda)—*Gopala Krishna*
ISBN: 81-7822-038-5 Code 0385

YOUR SUN SIGN AS A SPIRITUAL GUIDE—*J. Donald Walters (Kriyananda)*
ISBN: 81-7822-049-0 Code 0490